# THE FRAUDULENT TRANSFER HANDBOOK
## A Practical Guide For Lawyers andClients

ByEarl M. Forte

# THE FRAUDULENT TRANSFER HANDBOOK

by

Earl M. Forte

THE FRAUDULENT TRANSFER HANDBOOK –
A PRACTICAL GUIDE FOR LAWYERS AND CLIENTS
Copyright © 2017 by Earl M. Forte

This is a work of non-fiction.

All rights reserved. No part of this publication may be reproduced, stored in a retrieval system, or transmitted in any form or by any means without the prior written permission of the author, nor be otherwise circulated in any form of binding or cover other than that in which it is published.

*To Deborah, Thomas and Jonathan*

## Preface

This book is written to be used as a reference source for prosecuting and defending fraudulent transfer cases. And while it is not intended to be exhaustive of the subject of fraudulent transfer law, I have worked to make it comprehensive and clear to both practitionersand clients. Regardless of your level of knowledge or experience with the subject matter, you should find it useful.

## Chapter summaries

1.  **There is no "fraud" in a fraudulent transfer**

    With the occasional exception of claims brought against persons engaged in Ponzi schemes or other illicit activities, it is usually a misnomer to use the word "fraud" to describe what typically happens when there is a fraudulent transfer. This chapter discusses this definitional problem by comparing common law fraud, which focuses on compensating individual plaintiffs for harm caused to them by the defendant's misrepresentations, and fraudulent transfer law, which focuses on preserving the debtor's assets for the benefit of all the debtor's unsecured creditors.

2.  **Elements of a fraudulent transfer**

    This chapter contains a single checklist setting forth the elements of intentional and constructive fraudulent transfer claims under § 548 of the United States Bankruptcy Code, the Uniform Fraudulent Transfer Act and the older Uniform Fraudulent Conveyance Act.

3.  **What is a "transfer" or an "obligation"?**

    Chapter 3 defines a "transfer" and an "obligation", the first element of a fraudulent transfer claim. Both can be avoided and their value recovered for the benefit of the debtor's unsecured creditors.

4. **What is an "interest of the debtor in property"?**

    This chapter discusses the broad definition of "property" of the debtor, the second element of a fraudulent transfer claim, and some of the limits to that broad definition.

5. **What is "reasonably equivalent value" and "fair consideration"?**

    Chapter 4 discusses the phrase "reasonably equivalent value", as used in § 548 of the United States Bankruptcy Code and in the Uniform Fraudulent Transfer Act, and "fair consideration", the corresponding term used in the older Uniform Fraudulent Conveyance Act. These terms are used to measure the value of what the debtor received in exchange for the transfer or obligation. Both are required elements of a constructive fraudulent transfer claim and are also relevant to show intent to hinder, delay or defraud creditors in cases involving intentional fraudulent transfers.

6. **"Constructive" vs. "intentional" fraudulent transfers**

    This chapter discusses some of the major differences between claims for "constructive" and "intentional" (a/k/a "actual") fraudulent transfers. The chapter also addresses "badges of fraud", which are circumstances and factual scenarios from which intent to hinder, delay or defraud creditors can be inferred.

7. **The debtor's insolvency**

Chapter 7 reviews the standard for determining the insolvency of the debtor at the time of the transfer or obligation, or as a result of the transfer or obligation, both as a required element of a constructive fraudulent transfer claim and as a "badge of fraud" for an intentional fraudulent transfer claim.

8. **Tracing the property transferred**

This chapter discusses the requirement that the plaintiff trace the transfer of the debtor's property from the debtor to the initial transferee and to all subsequent transferees and how experts can be used to assist in this task.

9. **Bankruptcy Code vs. state law**

Chapter 9 discusses some of the most significant differences between the fraudulent transfer provisions in the United States Bankruptcy Code and state fraudulent transfer statutes.

10. **Reach back and limitations periods**

This chapter discusses the two-year reach back period that applies to fraudulent transfer claims under § 548 of the United States Bankruptcy Code and the four-year (or longer) reach back period that applies to claims under state fraudulent transfer statutes. The statutes of limitations and the doctrine of equitable tolling are also discussed.

**11. Who can sue to recover fraudulent transfers?**

Chapter 11 identifies the parties who are authorized to bring fraudulent transfer claims.

**12. Who can be sued to recover fraudulent transfers?**

This chapter identifies the parties who can be sued for the avoidance and recovery of fraudulent transfers.

**13. How much money can be recovered?**

Chapter 13 discusses how much a plaintiff can recover in damages in a fraudulent transfer case.

**14. Writing the complaint**

Chapter 14 sets forth the requirements for pleading a fraudulent transfer claim and directs the reader to several complaints in the public record as examples.

**15. Defending**

This chapter discusses strategies used to defend against fraudulent transfer claims by attacking the plaintiff's *prima facie* case, by attacking the plaintiff's standing to sue and by raising the good faith defense. There is also a short discussion about the limits on the bankruptcy court's authority to enter final orders and judgments in fraudulent transfer cases, notably in light of the Supreme Court's decision in *Stern v. Marshall*, 131 S. Ct. 2595 (2011).

### 16. Ponzi scheme problems

Chapter 16 discusses some of the effects a Ponzi scheme can have on fraudulent transfer claims.

### 17. The bar against constructive fraudulent transfer claims in § 546(e) of the Bankruptcy Code

This chapter discusses the bar to constructive fraudulent transfer claims in the "safe harbor" of § 546(e) of the United States Bankruptcy Code.

### 18. Is contribution or indemnification available?

Chapter 18 discusses whether common law rights of contribution and/or indemnification can be asserted by defendants in fraudulent transfer cases.

### 19. Is there directors and officers liability insurance coverage?

In this chapter, the book discusses whether a defendant in a fraudulent transfer case can expect to recover costs of defense and liability coverage under a directors and officers liability insurance policy.

### 20. The role of experts

Chapter 20 contains a general discussion about the role of experts in fraudulent transfer cases (for plaintiffs and defendants) and identifies subject areas that typically require expert assistance.

**21. Jury trials vs. non-jury trials**

This chapter discusses the availability of jury trials in fraudulent transfer actions filed in bankruptcy cases and what parties in bankruptcy cases should do to protect their jury trial right.

**22. Bankruptcy courts vs. other courts**

Chapter 22 discusses some of the perceived differences between United States bankruptcy courts, United States district courts and state courts as forums for fraudulent transfer cases. This chapter also discusses the power of the United States district court to withdraw the bankruptcy reference and transfer a fraudulent transfer case from the bankruptcy court to the district court for adjudication.

**23. A special problem – related criminal proceedings**

This chapter discusses the potential impact of a related criminal investigation or proceeding on fraudulent transfer litigation, notably the impact of Fifth Amendment privilege assertions and criminal guilty pleas and convictions.

**24.     Pre-complaint discovery under Fed. R. Bankr. P. 2004**

Chapter 24 discusses the ability of trustees and other parties-in-interest in bankruptcy cases, to use Rule 2004 of the Federal Rules of Bankruptcy Procedure to obtain documentary and testimonial evidence before filing a fraudulent transfer complaint.

**25.     Budgeting**

This chapter discusses budgeting in fraudulent transfer cases.

## CONTENTS

                                                               **Page**

Preface .................................................................................. 1
Chapter summaries ............................................................ 2
1. There is no "fraud" in a fraudulent transfer ................. 11
2. Elements of a fraudulent transfer ................................. 18
3. What is a "transfer" or an "obligation"? ...................... 22
4. What is "an interest of the debtor in property"? .......... 26
5. What is "reasonably equivalent value" and "fair consideration"? ............................................................... 32
6. "Constructive" vs. "intentional" fraudulent transfers ..... 38
7. The debtor's insolvency ................................................. 42
8. Tracing the property transferred ................................... 48
9. Bankruptcy Code vs. state law ...................................... 52
10. Reach back and limitations periods ............................. 57
11. Who can sue to recover fraudulent transfers? ............ 62
12. Who can be sued to recover fraudulent transfers? ..... 67
13. How much money can be recovered? ......................... 70
14. Writing the complaint .................................................. 73
15. Defending ....................................................................... 79
      a. Attacking the plaintiff's *prima facie* case ............ 80
      b. Attacking the plaintiff's standing to sue ............... 84
      c. The "good faith" defense ......................................... 87
      d. A procedural point for bankruptcy cases – final orders and judgments ............................................. 89
16. Ponzi scheme problems ................................................ 93

17. The bar against constructive fraudulent transfer claims in § 546(e) of the Bankruptcy Code .................... 100

18. Is contribution or indemnification available? .............. 103

19. Is there directors and officers liability insurance coverage? ................................................................. 107

20. The role of experts ....................................................... 111

21. Jury trials vs. non-jury trials ......................................... 114

22. Bankruptcy courts vs. other courts ............................... 118

      a. Withdrawal of the bankruptcy reference ........... 120

23. A special problem – related criminal proceedings ...... 124

24. Pre-complaint discovery under Fed. R. Bankr. P. 2004 ............................................................................ 127

25. Budgeting .................................................................... 130

Table of Authorities ........................................................ - 134 -

Index .................................................................................. - 154 -

About the Author ................................................................ 161

# 1.

**There is no "fraud" in a fraudulent transfer**

When clients find themselves sued by trustees or other plaintiffs for the avoidance and recovery of fraudulent transfers, they are sometimes surprised by the suggestion that they participated in a "fraud". This surprise is understandable. It is rooted in a misnomer.

The principal goal of fraudulent transfer law as codified in the United States Bankruptcy Code (the "Bankruptcy Code"), where it is so-often encountered, is *not* to compensate victims of "fraud", as "fraud" is commonly understood, but rather to preserve the debtor's assets for the collective benefit of all the debtor's unsecured creditors. *Buncher v. Official Committee of Unsecured Creditors of Genfarm LP IV*, 229 F. 3d 245, 250 (3d Cir. 2000); *Haskell v. PWS Holding Corporation (In re PWS Holding Corporation, et al.),*

303 F. 3d 308, 313 (3d Cir. 2002) *cert. denied, Haskell v. PWS Holding Corp.*, 123 S Ct. 1594 (2003); *Wiscovitch-Rentas v. Venancio Marti Santa, et al. (In re Laser Realty, Inc.)*, 2011 WL 2292269 at *4 (Bankr. P.R. 2011) (fraudulent transfers must diminish the debtor's funds); *National Labor Relations Board v. Arsham*, 873 F.2d 884, 887 (6th Cir. 1989); *Granfinanciera, S.A. v. Nordberg*, 492 U.S. 33, 56 (1989)(fraudulent transfer claims are brought by bankruptcy trustees to augment the bankruptcy estate); *Max Sugarman v. A.D.B. Investors, et al.*, 926 F.2d 1248, 1254 (1st Cir. 1991); *G.E. Credit Corp. v. Murphy(In re Rodriguez)*, 895 F.2d 725, 727 (11th Cir. 1990).[1]

Given this goal of asset preservation, it is a misnomer to use the word "fraud" to describe these avoidance claims. Nevertheless, the nasty "f" word is used to do just that in both the Bankruptcy Code and in many state fraudulent transfer statutes. *E.g.*, 11 U.S.C. § 548, "Fraudulent transfers and obligations"; 6 Del. C. § 1301, *et seq.*, Delaware "Uniform Fraudulent Transfer Act"; Cal. Civ. Code § 3439.01, *et-seq.*,California "Uniform Fraudulent Transfer Act"; 12 Pa.

---

[1] Unlike the Bankruptcy Code, New York's older Uniform Fraudulent Conveyance Act has been described as a set of legal rather than equitable doctrines, whose purpose is to aid specific creditors who have been defrauded by the transfer of a debtor's property, rather than to provide equal distribution of a debtor's estate among creditors. *Christian Brothers High School Endowment v. Bayou No Leverage Fund, LLC, et al. (In re Bayou Group, LLC, et al.)*, 439 B.R. 284, 303 (S.D.N.Y. 2010).

C.S. § 5101, *et seq.*; Pennsylvania "Uniform Fraudulent Transfer Act"; *Cf.* New York Debtor and Creditor Law §§ 270-281.

To compound the misnomer, fraudulent transfer law further provides that when determining actual intent to hinder, delay or defraud creditors, the fraudulent intent that is relevant is not the fraudulent intent of the defendant, but the fraudulent intent of the transferor/debtor, who in most cases is represented by the plaintiff — typically a bankruptcy trustee or debtor-in-possession.[2] In fact, fraudulent transfer law imposes no requirement that the defendant engage in any "fraud", dishonesty or other wrongful conduct to be found liable. *See, e.g., August v. August*, 2009 Del. Ch. LEXIS 21 at *35-*36 (Del. Ch. 2009) ("In cases of improperly transferred assets, the recipient of the transfer need not have engaged in wrongful conduct in order to owe restitution to the third party who was the victim of the transfer"); *Schock v. Nash*, 732 A.2d 217, 232 (Del. 1999)("Restitution is permitted even when the defendant retaining the benefit is not a wrong doer"); 11 U.S.C. § 548 (a)(1)(A) ("if the *debtor* made

---

[2] In fraudulent transfer actions filed in non-bankruptcy, non-receivership cases, the plaintiff will likely be an unsecured creditor of the debtor. 6 Del. C. § 1304(a); Cal. Civ. Code § 3439.04(a); 12 Pa. C.S. § 5104(a); New York Debtor and Creditor Law §§ 273, 274. Other parties may also become authorized to assert fraudulent transfer claims. *See* Chapter 11, Who can sue to recover fraudulent transfers?, *infra*.

such transfer or incurred such obligation with actual intent to hinder, delay or defraud")(emphasis added.)

Rather, to be found liable on a fraudulent transfer claim, the defendant need only (1) receive a transfer of the debtor's property (or benefit from a transfer of the debtor's property or an obligation incurred by the debtor) during the required time period, (2) by which the *debtor* intended to hinder, delay or defraud its unsecured creditors by transferring the property beyond their reach, or (3) for which transfer or obligation the debtor did not receive reasonably equivalent value (or fair consideration in good faith) in exchange, and (4) the transfer or obligation occurred when the debtor was insolvent or caused the debtor to become insolvent and unable to pay its creditors under various tests. *Buncher Co. v. Official Committee of Unsecured Creditors of Genfarm LP, IV*, 229 F.3d at 250;*Sharp International Corp v. State Street Bank and Trust (In re Sharp International Corp.)*, 403 F.3d 43, 56 (2d Cir. 2005). *See* Chapter 2, Elements of a fraudulent transfer, *infra*.

If the plaintiff prevails at trial, the property transferred, or its value in money (measured as of the date of the transfer or obligation), is returned to the debtor. If the plaintiff succeeds in avoiding an "obligation", the obligation is either cancelled and/or its value in money is returned to the debtor. And while the defendant in a fraudulent transfer case may receive credit for any value it provided to the debtor in exchange for the transfer or obligation (as the equities of the case may require), no credit will be given to the defendant for any value provided if the *debtor*, in making the transfer or incurring the obligation, acted intentionally to "hinder, delay or defraud" its unsecured creditors.[3] All funds restored to the debtor or its estate in a fraudulent transfer case must be used to benefit the debtor's unsecured creditors and cannot be used for other purposes. 6 Del. C. §§ 1307, 1308; *August v. August, et al.*, 2009 Del. Ch. LEXIS 21 at *33-34; *Voest-Alpine Trading USA Corp. v. Vantage Steel Corp.*, 919 F.2d 206, 214-18 (3d Cir. 1990); 11 U.S.C. § 548 (a)(1)(A); 6 Del. C. § 1304(a)(1); *In re Sharp International*, 403 F.3d at 56.

Thus, the "fraud" that the plaintiff must prove in a fraudulent transfer case is *not* necessarily fraud perpetrated against the plaintiff by the defendant, but rather a form of general business fraud, presumed in law to be perpetrated against all of the debtor's unsecured creditors by virtue of the intentional or unwise transfer of the debtor's property over certain time periods, usually during times of financial distress for the debtor. *In re Bayou Group, LLC, et al.*, 439 B.R.

---

[3]*See* Chapter 15, Defending, *infra*.

284, 304-05; *Melamed v. Lake County National Bank*, 727 F.2d 1399, 1401 (6th Cir. 1974); 5 Collier on Bankruptcy ¶ 548.04[1] (15th ed. rev. 2006); *Tiab Communications Corp. v. Keymarket of NEPA, Inc., et al.*, 263 F. Supp. 2d 925, 934-35 (M.D. Pa. 2003). *Cf.Coffey v. Foamex, L.P.*, 2 F.3d 157, 161-62 (6th Cir. 1993); *Global Link Liquidating Trust, etc. v. Avantel, S.A. (In re Global Link Telecom Corp., et al.)*, 327 B.R. 711, 717-18 (Bankr. D. Del. 2005)(Common law fraud requires the plaintiff to prove that the defendant engaged in intentional misrepresentations to the plaintiff of present or past material facts, with intent to deceive, reasonable reliance on those misrepresentations by the plaintiff, resulting in monetary damage to the plaintiff).

This "fraud by implication", if you will, is reflected in the types of evidence that courts will accept in fraudulent transfer cases to prove actual intent to "hinder, delay or defraud" creditors. Unlike common law fraud, which requires direct proof of fraudulent acts committed by the defendant against the plaintiff, evidence of fraudulent intent in fraudulent transfer cases is indirect and circumstantial, often referred to as "badges of fraud", which are circumstances and factual scenarios from which actual intent to "hinder, delay or defraud" creditors will be inferred.4 For constructive fraudulent transfer claims, the plaintiff is only required to prove that the debtor was insolvent at the time of the transfer or obligation (or became insolvent as a result of the transfer or obligation) and that reasonably equivalent value (or fair consideration in good faith) was not received by the debtor in exchange for the transfer or obligation. No proof of actual intent is required. *Id.*; 11 U.S.C. § 548(a)(1); 6 Del. C. § 1304(a); Cal Civ. Code §§ 3439.04(a)(2), 3439.05; 12 Pa. C. S. §§ 5104(a)(2), 5105; *e.g., Michaelson, as Trustee of the Appleseed's Litigation Trust v. Golden Gate Equity, Inc., et al. (In re Appleseed's Intermediate Holdings, LLC, et al.)*, Adversary No. 11-51847-KG, Docket No. 1 at 12-36 (Bankr. D. Del. 2011) (complaint seeking to avoid transfers and obligations based on claims for intentional and constructive fraudulent transfers under state law).

---

[4] *See* discussion below on "badges of fraud" in Chapter 6, "Constructive" vs. "intentional" fraudulent transfers, *infra*.

# 2.

**Elements of a fraudulent transfer**

With chapter 1 in mind, a plaintiff must allege and prove the following elements to prevail on a fraudulent transfer claim[5]:

(1) the existence of a transfer of an interest of the debtor in property, or the incurrence of an obligation by the debtor, that occurred within the applicable reach-back period (two years from the date of the filing of the debtor's bankruptcy petition for claims brought under § 548 of the Bankruptcy Code, four years, sometimes longer, from the date of the filing of the debtor's bankruptcy petition for claims

---

[5] While this checklist is designed to capture the elements of both intentional and constructive fraudulent transfer claims under the Bankruptcy Code and state fraudulent transfer statutes that follow the Uniform Fraudulent Transfer Act (the "UFTA") and the older Uniform Fraudulent Conveyance Act (the "UFCA"), practitioners should consult controlling state law for possible variations and nuance.

brought under state law pursuant to § 544 of the Bankruptcy Code, or four years, sometimes longer, from the date suit is filed by a creditor under a state fraudulent transfer statute, unless extended by equitable tolling);

(2) made or incurred by the debtor, either voluntarily or involuntarily, with actual intent to hinder, delay or defraud the debtor's present or future creditors; or

(3) for which the debtor received less than reasonably equivalent value (or "fair consideration" in good faith under the older UFCA, still in effect in a number of states, including New York) in exchange; and

(4) that was made or incurred when the debtor was insolvent or that caused the debtor to become insolvent; or

(5) at the time of the transfer or obligation the debtor was engaged in a business or transaction, or was about to engage in a business or transaction, for which the capital remaining with the debtor was unreasonably small; or

(6) at the time of the transfer or obligation the debtor intended to incur or believed that it would incur debts beyond its ability to pay those debts as they came due.

11 U.S.C. § 548(a)(1); 6 Del. C. §§ 1304, 1305; Cal. Civil Code §§ 3439.04, 3439.05; 12 Pa. C.S. §§ 5104, 5105; New York Debtor and Creditor Law §§ 271-276.

If a claim for "actual" (a/k/a "intentional") fraudulent transfers is alleged and proven by the plaintiff (elements (1) and (2) above), then reasonably equivalent value or fair consideration and insolvency (elements (3), (4), (5) and (6) above) do not have to be proven for the plaintiff to prevail.[6] *See* 11 U.S.C. § 548(a)(1)(A); 6 Del. C. § 1304(a)(1); 12 Pa. C.S. § 5104(a); *Mitchell v. Wilmington Trust Co.*, 449 A.2d 1055 (Del. Ch. 1982); *United States v. Green*, 201 F.3d 251 (3d Cir. 2000); *In re Bayou Group, LLC*, 439 B.R. at 330. However, the presence of insolvency or the absence of reasonably equivalent value or fair consideration can also be used to prove fraudulent intent, since they are also considered to be "badges of fraud". *See* Chapter 6, "Constructive" vs. "intentional" fraudulent transfers, *infra* at 41 n.11.

On the other hand, if a claim for "constructive" fraud is asserted by the plaintiff, then the plaintiff must only prove that the debtor did not receive "reasonably equivalent value"

---

[6] In addition, fraudulent transfer claims based on payments made to an insider of the debtor that were not made in the ordinary course of business, do not require proof of the debtor's insolvency. 11 U.S.C. § 548(a)(1)(B)(ii)(IV); *Stanley v. U.S. Bank, National Association (In re TransTexas Gas Corp.)*, 597 F.3d 298, 308 (5th Cir. 2010). Some state fraudulent transfer statutes modify this standard for so-called "insider" fraudulent transfers by requiring that the plaintiff allege and prove that the debtor was insolvent at the time of the transfer to the insider and that the insider had "reasonable cause to believe" that the debtor was insolvent at the time the debtor made the transfer to him. *E.g.*, 6 Del. C. § 1305(b); Annotated Laws of Massachusetts, General Law ch. 109A, § 6(b) (2010).

(or "fair consideration" in good faith under the UFCA) in exchange for the transfer or obligation and was insolvent when the transfer was made or obligation incurred, or became insolvent as a result of the transfer or obligation (elements (3) and either, (4), (5) or (6) above). 11 U.S.C. § 548(a)(1)(B)(i) and (ii); 6 Del. C. §§ 1304(a)(2), 1305(a); Cal. Civ. Code §§ 3439.04, 3439.05; 12 Pa. C.S. §§ 5104, 5105; New York Debtor and Creditor Law § 272; *Calvert v. Radford (In re Consolidated Meridian Funds, a/k/a Meridian Investors Trust, et al.)*, --B.R.--, 2013 WL 366233 (Bankr. W.D.Wash. 2013) (trustee has burden of proving all elements of a fraudulent transfer). [7]

---

[7] While statistics have not been gathered and analyzed on this point for purposes of this writing, anecdotally, it appears to the author that claims for "constructive" fraudulent transfers may be more common than claims for "actual" (a/k/a "intentional") fraudulent transfers, especially in bankruptcy cases. This could be explained by the steeper level of proof required to show "actual" intent to hinder, delay or defraud, which requires proof of more than one "badge of fraud" by clear and convincing evidence. *E.g.,see National Loan Investors, L.P. v. LAN Associates XII, LLP*, 2002 Conn. Super. LEXIS 2233 (Conn. Super. Ct. 2002); *Murphy v. Meritor Savings Bank (In re O'Day Corporation)*, 126 B.R. 370, 410 (Bank. D. Mass. 1991). Elements of a constructive fraudulent transfer generally must be proven only by a preponderance of the evidence. *Committee of Unsecured Creditors for Pittsburgh Cut Flower Company, Inc. v. Hoopes (In re Pittsburgh Cut Flower Company, Inc.)*, 124 B.R. 451, 456 (Bankr. W.D. Pa. 1991); *see generally* 4 Collier on Bankruptcy § 548.10 (15$^{th}$ ed. 1990). If the plaintiff proves the elements of a constructive fraudulent transfer, a conclusive presumption of fraud arises. *In re Pittsburgh Cut Flower Company, Inc.*, 124 B.R. at 456.

# 3.

### What is a "transfer" or an "obligation"?

The word "transfer" is defined in § 101(54) of the Bankruptcy Code as the "creation of a lien, the retention of title as a security interest, the foreclosure of a debtor's equity of redemption or each mode, direct or indirect, absolute or conditional, voluntary or involuntary, of disposing of or parting with property or an interest in property". 11 U.S.C. § 101(54). The definition of "transfer" in the UFTA as adopted in most states is essentially the same. *E.g.*, 6 Del. C. § 1301(12); Cal. Civ. Code § 3439.01(i) (2011); 12 Pa. C.S. § 5101(b); *Black & White Cattle Co. v. Granada Cattle Services, Inc. (In re Black & White Cattle Co.)*, 783 F.2d 1454, 1462 (9th Cir. 1986).

"Transfers" can consist of transfers of cash, the granting of a security interest in the debtor's property, or other property dispositions. *IBT International, Inc., et al. v. Northern* (*In re International Administrative Services, Inc.*), 408 F.3d 689, 696-97 (11th Cir. 2008) (cash transfers); *Rubin v. Manufacturers Hanover Trust Co.*, 661 F.2d 979, 991 (2d Cir. 1981) (giving collateral to secure a loan is a "transfer"); *Osage Crude Oil Purchasing, Inc. v. Osage Oil and Transportation, Inc.* (*In re Osage Crude Oil Purchasing, Inc.*), 103 B.R. 256, 262 (Bankr. N. D. Okla. 1989) (creation of a security interest is a "transfer".)

In some cases, courts may "collapse" multiple transfers for fraudulent transfer purposes, treating a number of transfers as effectively one. *Voest-Alpine Trading USA Corp. v. Vantage SteelCorp*, 919 F.2d at 211-13; *Hechinger Investment Co. of DE v. Fleet Retail Finance Group* (*In re-Hechinger Investment Co. of DE*), 327 B.R. 537, 546 (Bankr. D. Del. 2005)*citingUnited States v. Tabor Court Realty Corp., et al.*, 803 F.2d 1288, 1299 n.4, 1302 (3d Cir. 1986) (court collapsed two separate loan transactions based on a showing of, among other things, an absence of fair consideration and good faith under the former Pennsylvania UFCA); *Brandt v. B.A. Capital Company LP* (*In re Plassein Int'l. Corp., et al.*), 366 B.R. 318, 326 (Bankr D. Del. 2007).

The term "obligation" is not defined in the Bankruptcy Code or in the UFTA and appears to be the subject of little discussion in the case law. Black's Law Dictionary defines "obligation" as "[a] generic word, derived from the Latin substantive 'obligator', having many, wide and varied meanings, according to the context in which it is used. That which a person is bound to do or forbear; any duty imposed by law, promise, contract, relations of society, courtesy, kindness, etc. (citations omitted)." Black's Law Dictionary (5th Ed. 1979). Indeed, what constitutes an "obligation" seems self-evident. Obligations are incurred, for purposes of fraudulent transfer claims, on the date when the debtor borrows under a loan or other obligation. *In re Osage Crude Oil Purchasing, Inc.*, 103 B.R. at 262; *In re O'Day Corporation*, 126 B.R. at 372 (avoidance of liens and security interests under the UFCA).

The plaintiff in a fraudulent transfer case must not only plead and prove the existence of a transfer or obligation, but must also identify the specific dates on which the transfers were made or the obligation incurred. This is necessary for a number of reasons, including: determining if the transfer or obligation took place within the applicable reach-back period (*see* Chapter 10, Reach back periods and limitations periods, *infra*); to identify all transferees subject to suit; to determine the dates on which reasonably equivalent value, fair consideration and insolvency must be measured; and to calculate the amount of damages the plaintiff may recover measured by the monetary value of all transfers or obligations on the date they occurred. *Leonard v. Coolidge, et al. (In re National Audit Defense Network)*, 367 B.R. 207, 219 (Bankr. D. Nev. 2007) (discussing the trustee's evidence and describing the transfers the trustee was seeking to recover).

# 4.

**What is "an interest of the debtor in property"?**

What is "property" or "an interest of the debtor in property" that must be the subject of a transfer or obligation such that the plaintiff can seek to avoid its transfer and recover its value? The answer is straight forward enough - just about anything that can be owned. This very broad definition of "property", which is derived from the statutes and case law, does, however, have limits.

Looking first to the statutes; in bankruptcy cases "property" of the debtor's estate is defined in § 541 of the Bankruptcy Code as "[a]ll legal or equitable interests of the debtor in property as of the commencement of the case" and includes "[a]ny interest in property that the trustee recovers under section … 550…of this title", e.g., property recovered in fraudulent transfer litigation. 11 U.S.C. §§ 541(a)(1), (3); *seeBegier v. I.R.S.*, 496 U.S. 53, 59 n. 3 (1990). State fraudulent transfer statutes that follow the UFTA define "property" even more broadly as "anything that may be the subject of ownership". 6 Del. C. § 1301(10); Cal. Civ. Code § 3439.01(h); 12 Pa. C.S. § 5101(b); *3V Capital Masters Fund, Ltd., et al. v. Official Committee of Unsecured Creditors of Tousa, Inc., et al. (In re Tousa, Inc.)*, 444 B.R. 613, 656 (S.D. Fla. 2011) *rev'd* at 680 F.3d 1298 (11th Cir. 2012) (noting that "property" is used consistently throughout the Bankruptcy Code in its broadest sense, including cash, all interests in property, such as liens, and every kind of consideration, including promises to act or forebear); *McHale v. Boulder Capital, LLC, et al. (In re The 1031 Exchange Group LLC, et al.)*, 439 B.R. 47, 70 (Bankr. S.D.N.Y. 2010)("money in a bank account in the name of the debtor is presumed to be property of the bankruptcy estate"); 5 Collier on Bankruptcy ¶ 541.08 ("Deposits in the debtor's bank account become property of the estate under section 541(a)(1)"); *Segal v. Rochelle*, 382 U.S. 375, 379, (1966) ("[t]he term 'property' has been construed most generously and an interest is not outside its reach because it is novel or contingent or because enjoyment must be postponed"); *United States v. Whiting Pools, Inc.*, 462 U.S. 198, 204-05 (1983). ("[P]roperty of the estate" includes contract rights). *EBC I, Inc. v. America Online Inc. (In re EBC I, Inc., et al.)*, 356 B.R. 631, 639 (Bankr. D. Del. 2006).

What exactly constitutes a "property interest" under the broad definition in the Bankruptcy Code and the UFTA, is generally determined by state law, even in cases brought under the Bankruptcy Code – "[p]roperty interests", are created and defined by state law "[u]less some federal interest requires a different result, there is no reason why such interests should be analyzed differently simply because an interested party is involved in a bankruptcy proceeding." *Travelers Casualty & Surety Co. of America v. Pacific Gas & Elec. Co.*, 549 U.S. 443, 451 (1979); *Butner v. United States*, 440 U.S. 48, 55 (1979).

Therefore, a threshold issue in fraudulent transfer litigation is whether "an interest of the debtor in property" was transferred. *In re Tousa, Inc.*, 444 B.R. 646; *Golden v. The Guardian (In re Lenox Healthcare, Inc.)*, 343 B.R. 96, 100 (Bankr. D. Del. 2006). To prove this, the plaintiff must prove that at the time of the transfer the debtor had sufficient dominion and control over the property to claim ownership, meaning that the debtor had the power to designate freely who would receive the property and to disburse the property to that person. *In re Tousa, Inc.*, 444 B.R. at 647;

*Nordberg v. Sanchez (In re Chase & Sanborn Corp.)*, 813 F.2d 1177, 1199 (11th Cir. 1987); *Howdeshell of Ft. Myers v. Dunham-Bush, Inc. (In re Howdeshell of Fort Myers)*, 55 B.R. 470, 474-75 (Bankr. M.D. Fla. 1985) (control by the debtor over the property does not exist where a loan from a third party required the debtor to pay the loan proceeds to a particular creditor). "[I]f the debtor transfers property that would not have been available for distribution to his creditors in a bankruptcy proceeding, the policy behind the avoidance power is not implicated." *Begier v. I.R.S.*, 496 U.S. at 58.

If the debtor is a "mere conduit" or "financial intermediary" with respect the property, or holds "bare legal title" to the property for the benefit of another, or if the property transferred by the debtor was previously "earmarked" to go from the debtor to another party, then the debtor will likely be deemed not to have an interest in the property sufficient to support a claim for its recovery as a fraudulent transfer. *In re Chase & Sanborn Corp.*, 813 F.2d at 1180-82 (mere conduit); *Ogden v. Big Sky Motors, Ltd.*, 314 F. 3d 1190, 1196 (10th Cir. 2002) (financial conduit); *Cooper v. Centar Investments (Asia) Ltd., et al. (In re Trigem America Corporation)*, 431 B.R. 855, 860 (Bankr. C.D. Cal. 2010) (earmarking, mere conduit); *Kapila v. Espirito Santo Bank (In* re *Bankfest Capital Corp.*), 374 B.R. 333 (Bankr. S.D. Fla. 2007) (control test); *In re Lenox Healthcare, Inc.*, 343 B.R. at 100 (property held by the debtor in trust for another gives the debtor bare legal title and no property interest); *Lyon v. Contech Construction Products, Inc.* (*In re Computrex, Inc.*), 403 F.3d 807, 810-13 (6th Cir. 2005) (the debtor was contractually bound to hold the transferred funds for the benefit of another party and to pay those funds to that third party and therefore lacked a property interest in the funds)[8]; *Stoebner v. Consumer Energy Company* (*In re LGI Energy Solutions, Inc., et al.*), 460 B.R. 720, 729-30 (8th Cir. B.A.P. 2011) (property held by the debtor that had been segregated and identified in a bailment arrangement for the benefit of another party, was not property of the debtor's estate under state bailment law).

Thus, "property of the estate" or "property of the debtor", although very broadly defined, has limits and does not necessarily include all property that happens to come in-

---

[8] The Sixth Circuit's decision in *Computrex* raises the question of how to determine property interests in funds the debtor holds for the benefit of others when those funds are commingled with funds belonging to multiple parties. *In re Computrex, Inc.*, 403 F.3d at 811-12. In *Computrex* the Sixth Circuit concluded that the debtor's commingling of funds did not override the requirement in the debtor's contract with its customer that the funds were to be paid over to a third party and stated "we will not condone a debtor's improper application of funds to justify that the funds were property of the debtor's estate." *Id.* at 812-13. *SeealsoWeiner v. A.G. Minzer Supply Corp.* (*In re UDI Corporation*), 301 B.R. 104, 114-15 (Bankr. D. Mass. 2003).

to the debtor's possession. Plaintiffs should be certain of the debtor's interest in the property transferred before filing suit and defendants should examine this issue closely and raise all available arguments to attack the plaintiff's claim to ownership of the property transferred. Parties should be aware of the various tests that courts apply when deciding this issue.[9]

---

[9] The "control", "mere conduit", "financial intermediary" and "earmarking" theories, can also be used by defendants to argue that they did not acquire an interest in property they received from the debtor and therefore cannot be a "transferee" with fraudulent transfer liability. *E.g., Christy v. Alexander & Alexander of New York, Inc., et al.* (*In re Finley, Kumble, et al.*), 130 F.3d 52, 55-59 (2d Cir. 1997); *Goldman Sachs Execution & Clearing, L.P., et al. v. The Official Unsecured Creditors Committee of Bayou Group LLC, et al.*, 2012 U.S. App. LEXIS 13531 at *6-*8 (2d Cir. 2012); *Ogden v. Big Sky Motors, Ltd.*, 314 F. 3d at 1196 (financial conduit); *Paloian v. LaSalle Bank, N.A.*, 619 F. 2d 688, 691 (7thCir. 2010) (when a check written by the debtor transfers money from the debtor to the checking account of a bank's customer, the customer, not the bank, is the initial transferee, because the bank simply holds the funds for the customer's benefit). *See* Chapter 15, Defending, *infra*.

# 5.

## What is "reasonably equivalent value" and "fair consideration"?

"[R]easonably equivalent value" is not defined in the Bankruptcy Code. Congress left that task to the courts. *See Mellon Bank, N.A. v. Official Committee of Unsecured Creditors of R.M.L., Inc. (In re R.M.L., Inc.)*, 92 F.3d 139, 148 (3d Cir. 1996); *Cooper v. Ashley Communications (In re Morris Communications NC, Inc.)*, 914 F.2d 458, 466 (4th Cir. 1990). While § 548(d)(2)(A) of the Bankruptcy Code defines "value" as "property, or satisfaction or securing of a present or antecedent debt of the debtor, but does not include an unperformed promise to furnish support to the debtor or a relative of the debtor", this definition has limited use when determining whether "reasonably equivalent value" or "fair consideration" was received for purposes of fraudulent transfer claims and hence courts treat the issue of reasonably equivalent value or fair consideration as a factual question to be determined by the unique circumstances of each case. *See Barber v. Gold Seed Co.*, 129 F.3d 382, 387 (7th Cir. 1997); *In re TransTexas Group Corp., et al.*, 597 F.3d at 306; *In re Tousa, Inc.*, 444 B.R. at 649-50, 662; 11 U.S.C. § 548(d)(2)(A); *In re Sharp International Corp.*, 403 F. 3d at 53-54 (There are three elements to "fair consideration" within the meaning of New York constructive fraudulent transfer law: (1) the recipient of the alleged fraudulent transfer must either convey property or discharge an antecedent debt in exchange; (2) the exchange must be for a fair equivalent; and (3) the exchange must be in good faith).

Despite the factual nature of the inquiry, some general parameters for determining "reasonably equivalent value" or "fair consideration" have emerged from case law. First, reasonably equivalent value is measured as of the date of the transfer or obligation, rarely at another time or from hindsight, and it is determined from the standpoint of the debtor's unsecured creditors. *In re TransTexas Group Corp., et al.*, 597 F.3d at 306 *citingHinsley v. Boudloche (Inre Hinsley)*, 201 F.3d 638, 644 (5th Cir. 2000). "The proper focus [for determining whether reasonably equivalent value was received] is on the net effect of the transfers on the debtor's estate [and] the funds available to the unsecured creditors." *Id.*; *Allard v. Flamingo Hilton (In re Chomakos)*, 69 F.3d 769, 770-71 (6th Cir. 1995); *Butler Aviation International v. White (In re Fairchild Aircraft Corp.)*, 6 F.3d 1119, 1126 (5th Cir. 1993). The Supreme Court of the United States has stated that reasonably equivalent value is provided when "the debtor has received value that is substantially comparable to the worth of the transferred property." *BFP v. Resolution Trust Corp.*, 511 U.S. 531, 548 (1994); *see also Wyle v. C.H. Rider & Family (In re United Energy Corp.)*, 944 F.2d 589, 597 (9th Cir. 1991).

Reasonably equivalent value can be given to the debtor either directly or indirectly and can be in the form of a direct or indirect economic benefit. *Lisle v. John Wiley & Sons, Inc. (In re Wilkinson, et al.)*, 196 Fed. Appx. 337, 342 (6th Cir. 2006); *citing Rubin v. Manufacturers Hanover Trust Co.*, 661 F.2d at 991-92.

And while most courts reject a bright line, mathematical test for measuring reasonably equivalent value or fair consideration, focusing instead on an approximation of fair market value, some courts still apply the often criticized "70% benchmark rule" for measuring reasonably equivalent value. *See Jacoway v. Anderson, et al. (In re Ozark Restaurant Equipment Co.)*, 850 F.2d 342, 344 (8th Cir. 1988);

*Viscount Air Services, Inc. v. Cole, et al. (In re Viscount Air Services, Inc.)*, 232 B.R. 416, 435 (Bankr. D. Az. 1998); *Thrifty Dutchman, Inc. v. Florida Supermarkets, Inc. (In re Thrifty Dutchman, Inc.)*, 97 B.R. 101, 108 (Bankr. S.D. Fla. 1998); *Durrett v. Washington National Ins. Co.*, 621 F.2d 201, 203 (5th Cir. 1980).

States that follow the UFTA apply the "reasonably equivalent value" standard, while states that still follow the older UFCA, such as New York, use the "fair consideration" standard. 6 Del. C. §§ 1304(a)(2), 1305 (follows UFTA); Cal. Civ. Code §§ 3439.04(a)(2), 3439.05 (follows UFTA); 12 Pa. C.S. §§ 5103 and Committee Comment, 5104 (a)(2), 5105 (follows UFTA); New York Debtor and Creditor Law §§ 272-275 (follows UFCA). *SeeHBE Leasing Corp. v. Frank*, 48 F.3d 623, 638-39 (2d Cir. 1995) ("to determine whether a debtor indirectly received fair consideration...the fact-finder must first attempt to measure the economic benefit that the debtor indirectly received from the entire transaction, and then compare that benefit to the value of the property the debtor transferred... The mere fact that the debtor received a benefit is therefore insufficient to find fair consideration"); *In re Sharp International Corp.*, 403 F.3d at 53-54. The principal difference between "reasonably equivalent value" and "fair consideration," is that "fair consideration" contains a good faith element, while "reasonably equivalent value" does not. New York Debtor and Creditor Law § 272; *Mendelsohn v. Jacobwitz, et al. (In re Jacobs)*, 394 B.R. 646, 660 (Bankr. E.D.N.Y. 2008).

The plaintiff in fraudulent transfer litigation has the burden of proving that reasonably equivalent value or fair consideration was not received by the debtor in exchange for the transfer or obligation. *In re Tousa, Inc.*, 444 B.R. at 613; *Braunstein v. Walsh (In re Rowanoak Corp.)*, 344 F.3d 126, 131 (1st Cir. 2003); *Dahar v. Jackson (In re Jackson)*, 459 F.3d 117, 121-23 (1st Cir. 2006) (state UFTA). Under the New York UFCA, the plaintiff also has the burden of proving that the transferee did not act in good faith. *In re Jacobs*, 394 B.R. at 660.

If the transfer or obligation and any value given in exchange are not in the form of cash, then parties in fraudulent transfer litigation must be prepared to present fact and expert opinions on the value to the property transferred and the value of the property received in exchange. The unique facts of each case and the characteristics of the particular property, will control. To avoid attacks from your opponent and the court, select an expert with specialized expertise in the particular property being valued. *E.g.TWA v. Travelers International AG (In re TWA)*, 180 B.R. 389, 416 (Bankr. D.

Del. 1994)*rev'd and aff'd in part*,134 F. 3d 188 (3d Cir. 1998).

# 6.

## "Constructive" vs. "intentional" fraudulent transfers

Thus, there are two general categories of fraudulent transfer claims – (1) claims based on "actual" or "intentional" fraud, which require the plaintiff to prove by clear and convincing evidence that in making the transfer or incurring the obligation, the transferor (the debtor in bankruptcy cases) actually intended to hinder, delay or defraud its unsecured creditors by placing the transferred property beyond their reach, and (2) claims based on "constructive" fraud, which do not require proof by the plaintiff of actual intent by the transferor/debtor to hinder, delay or defraud its creditors, but only proof that the debtor did not receive reasonably equivalent value or fair consideration in exchange for the transfers or obligations and that the transferor/debtor was insolvent at the time of the transfer or obligation or became insolvent as a result of the transfer or obligation. *See Official Committee of Unsecured Creditors of Verestar, Inc. v. Am. Tower Corp. (In re Verestar, Inc.)*, 343 B.R. 444, 460 (Bankr. S.D.N.Y 2006); *Daley, et al. v. Zofia Deptula, et al. (In re Carrozzella & Richardson)*, 286 B.R. 480, 483, n.3 (D. Conn. 2002); 11 U.S.C. § 548; 6 Del. C. § 1301, *et seq.*; Cal. Civ. Code § 3439.01, *et seq.*; 12 Pa. C.S. § 5101, *et seq.*; New York Debtor and Creditor Law § 270, *et seq.*

Because actual intent to hinder, delay or defraud creditors typically cannot be proven by direct evidence, the law permits the plaintiff to rely on circumstantial evidence of actual intent, which requires a showing by clear and convincing evidence of two or more "badges of fraud". 5 Collier on Bankruptcy, ¶ 548.04[2][a] at 548-23 to 548-24 (15th rev. ed. 1997); *Official Committee of Unsecured Creditors of Fedders North America, Inc., et al. v. Goldman Sachs Credit Partners, L.P., et al. (In re Fedders North America, Inc., et al.)*, 405 B.R. 527, 545 (Bankr. D. Del. 2009); *In re Sharp International Corp.*, 403 F.3d at 56.[10] The various enumer-

---

[10] If a Ponzi scheme was perpetrated by the transferor/debtor, then actual intent to hinder, delay or defraud creditors will be presumed. *In re Bayou Group, LLC*, 439 B.R. at 294, 305, 307; *Merrill v. Abbott (In re Independent Clearing House Company)*, 77 B.R. 843, 860-61 (D. Utah 1987); *AFI Holding, Inc. v. Mackenzie*, 525 F.3d 700, 704 (9th Cir. 2008) ("[T]he mere existence of a Ponzi scheme is sufficient to establish actual intent to hinder, delay or defraud"). *Cunningham v. Brown, et al.*, 265

ated examples of "badges of fraud" listed in state fraudulent transfer statutes and those identified in case law, are non-exclusive and any evidence that shows actual intent to hinder, delay or defraud that is relevant under the circumstances is generally admissible on this issue. *E.g.*, 6 Del. C. § 1304(b); Cal. Civ. Code § 3439.04(b); 12 Pa. C.S. § 5104(b), Committee Comment 5 (1993); *In re Sharp International Corp.*, 403 F.3d at 56.

The search for "badges of fraud" elicits a fact-driven, case-specific inquiry, with more liberality granted to trustees and other estate representatives, who typically lack personal knowledge of the facts. *United States v. Gleneagles Inv. Co., et al.*, 565 F. Supp. 556, 580 (M.D. Pa. 1983) *aff'd sub nom.*, *United States v. Tabor Court Realty Corp.*, 803 F.2d 1288 (3d Cir. 1986), *cert. denied* 483 U.S. 1005 (1987); *see also Pardo v. Avanti Corporate Health System (In re APF Co.)*, 274 B.R. 634, 638 (Bankr. D. Del. 2001) (noting that more liberality is given to trustees when pleading actual fraud); *Joseph v. Frank, et al. (In re Troll Communications)*, 385 B.R. 110, 124 (Bankr. D. Del. 2008). No single badge of fraud standing alone will establish actual fraudulent intent, how-

---

U.S. 1, 8, (1924) (original Ponzi case.); *In re National Audit Defense Network*, 367 B.R. at 221-23 (presence of "Ponzi like" scheme was sufficient to establish defendants' intent to hinder, delay or defraud creditors); *Plotkin v. Pomona Valley Imports, Inc. (In re Cohen)*, 199 B.R. 709, 717 (9th Cir. 1996).

ever, the presence of several will raise a presumption of fraudulent intent. *Fleming Companies, Inc. v. Rich*, 978 F. Supp. 1281, 1297-98 (E.D. Mo. 1997).[11]

---

[11]Examples of recognized badges of fraud include: the debtor's insolvency at or near the time of the transfer or obligation; the involvement of insiders of the debtor with the transfer or obligation; a close relationship between the debtor and the person or entity that received or benefitted from the transfer or obligation; insiders of the debtor benefitting in some way from the transfer or obligation; concealment of the transfer or obligation from creditors; the absence of reasonably equivalent value or fair consideration received by the transferor/debtor in exchange for the transfer or obligation; mounting litigation or collection efforts against the transferor/debtor by creditors at or near the time of the transfer or obligation; incurrence of a large debt near the time of the transfer; the presence of a criminal proceeding involving the debtor's or transferor's activities and the activities of insiders near the time of the transfer or obligation; knowledge of the debtor's insolvency by insiders at the time of the transfer or obligation; the presence or use of dummy corporations with little or no assets, operations or employees to receive or make the subject transfers; the presence of criminal guilty pleas or convictions of insiders of the debtor in matters related to the transfers or obligations; and all other facts that are relevant under the circumstances. 12 Pa. C.S. § 5104(b); Cal. Civ. Code § 3439.04; 6 Del. C. § 1304(b) (2011); Annotated Laws of Massachusetts, General Law ch. 109A, § 5(b) (2010); *Schilling v. Heavrin (In re Triple S Restaurants, Inc.)*, 422 F.3d 405, 414 (6th Cir. 2005); *In re Bayou Group, LLC, et al.*, 439 B.R. at 306, 307; *In re Sharp International Corp.*, 403 F.3d at 56; *Johnson, et al. v. Neilson (In re Slatkin)*, 525 F.3d 805 (9th Cir. 2008) (Ponzi scheme operator's guilty plea was admissible under F.R.E. 807 in a civil action for fraudulent transfers and conclusively established debtor's fraudulent intent).

# 7.

## The debtor's insolvency

As previously discussed, although the plaintiff is not required to prove the debtor's insolvency to avoid and recover a fraudulent transfer based on "actual" intent to hinder, delay or defraud creditors, the plaintiff is required to do so to recover a fraudulent transfer based on "constructive" fraud. 11 U.S.C. § 548(a)(1)(B); 6 Del. C. §§ 1304(a)(2), 1305; Cal. Civ. Code §§ 3439.04, 3439.05; 12 Pa. C.S. §§ 5104(a)(2), 5105. However, even in cases involving intentional (a/k/a "actual") fraudulent transfers, the issue of the debtor's insolvency is relevant as circumstantial evidence of actual intent, i.e., it is a "badge of fraud." 6 Del. C. § 1304(b)(9); Cal. Civ. Code § 3439.04(b)(9); 12 Pa. C.S. § 5104; *Max Sugarman Funeral Home, Inc. v. A.D.B. Investors*, 926 F.2d at 1254;*Official Committee of Unsecured Creditors of Midway*

*Games, Inc. v. National Amusements, Inc. (In re Midway Games, Inc.)*, 428 B.R. 303, 325 (Bankr. D. Del. 2010).

While recognizing the distinction between intentional and constructive fraud with respect to the issue of the debtor's insolvency, it is probably fair to say that fraudulent transfer claims, whether intentional or constructive, arise almost exclusively in circumstances of financial distress or insolvency for the debtor, meaning that the need to address the issue of the debtor's insolvency arises in most cases.[12]

How is the debtor's insolvency determined? While controlling local law should always be consulted on this issue, the insolvency of the debtor under the Bankruptcy Code and state fraudulent transfer statutes that follow UFTA, is typically proven by showing that at the time of the transfer or obligation, or as a result of the transfer or obligation, the sum of the debtor's debts exceeded its property, at fair value, excluding all exempt property and property transferred, concealed or removed with intent to hinder, delay or defraud creditors. 11 U.S.C. § 101(32); 6 Del. C. § 1302; Cal. Civ. Code

---

[12] The debtor's insolvency may also be presumed under certain circumstances. For example, if a Ponzi scheme is proven, this can give rise to a presumption that the debtor was insolvent when the transfers were made or the obligation incurred. *See* Chapter 16, Ponzi scheme problems, *infra*. A presumption of insolvency can also arise when there is an absence of fair consideration under the UFCA. *See In re Jacobs*, 394 B.R. at 672 ("Under New York law there is a presumption of insolvency where the debtor makes a transfer without fair consideration.").

§ 3439.02; 12 Pa. C.S. § 5102; *Coleman v. Home Savings Association (In re Coleman)*, 21 B.R. 832, 835 (Bankr. S.D. Tex. 1982). "Fair value" for insolvency purposes is determined from the view point of creditors and asks what is the value for which the debtor's assets could be converted into cash to pay creditors within a reasonable time. *In re TWA*, 180 B.R. at 411, citing *In re Coated Seals, Inc.*, 144 B.R. 663, 668 (Bankr. S.D.N.Y. 1992); *TWA v. Travellers International AG (In re TWA)*, 134 F.3d 188, 193-96 (3d Cir. 1998); *Covey v. Commercial National Bank of Peoria*, 960 F. 2d 657, 660 (7th Cir. 1992)("To decide whether a firm is insolvent within the meaning of § 548(a)(2)(B)(i), a court should ask: What would a buyer be willing to pay for the debtor's entire package of assets and liabilities? If the price is positive, the firm is solvent, if negative, insolvent".); *Gordon v. Kinney (In re Gallagher)*, 417 B.R. 677, 683 n. 5 (Bankr. W.D.N.Y. 2009) (when determining insolvency under § 271 of the New York Debtor and Creditor Law, the court adopted language used in 11 U.S.C. § 101 (32)(A), "which conforms to the balance sheet test for insolvency in a bankruptcy sense.").

Valuation can be premised either on "going-concern" or liquidation value. Going concern is equivalent to fair market value, while liquidation assumes a forced sale or distressed value. *Helig-Meyers Co. v. Wachovia Bank, N.A.(In re Helig-Meyers Co.)*, 328 B.R. 471, 477 (E.D. Va. 2005); *In re O'Day Corporation*, 126 B.R. at 402-03 (discusses "going concern" valuation compared to "present fair saleable value of . . . assets" under the UFCA).

While determining fair value based on the debtor's financial statements prepared in accordance with Generally Accepted Accounting Principles ("GAAP") is not relevant for determining insolvency in fraudulent transfer litigation, a GAAP financial statement for the debtor from a time near the date of the transfer or obligation, can be a useful starting point for an insolvency analysis. *In re TWA*, 180 B.R. at 404-05; *Kendall v. Sorani (In re Richmond Produce Co.)*, 151 B.R. 1012, 1019 (Bankr. N.D. Cal. 1993) *aff'd*, 195 B.R. 455 (N.D. Cal. 1996).

While assets are typically valued at "fair valuation", other methods can be used in different contexts. *In re TWA*, 180 B.R. at 411, n.8, 422-25. Debts, however, must be valued at their face amount, *not* at fair value. *In re Xonics Photochemical, Inc.*, 841 F.2d 198, 200 (7th Cir. 1988); *In re TWA*, 180 B.R. at 422-25; *Lids Corporation v. Marathon Investment Partners, L.P. (In re Lids Corp.)*, 281 B.R. 535, 545-46 (Bankr. D. Del. 2002).

Contingent liabilities and the overall economic context of the debtor's industry should also be considered when performing an insolvency analysis. *In re TWA*, 180 B.R. at 412-15; *Scholes v. Lehmann et al.*, 56 F.3d 750, 762 (7th Cir. 1995) (noting that contingent tort claims can create insolvency).

The older UFCA, still in use in a number of states, notably New York, uses a somewhat different test for measuring insolvency – "present fair saleable value", which means the value that can be achieved for assets sold reasonably promptly in an existing market. New York Debtor and Creditor Law § 271; *Corbin v. Franklin National Bank (In re Franklin National Bank Securities Litigation)*, 2 B.R. 687, 711 (E.D.N.Y. 1979); *Lippe, et al. v. Bairnco Corporation*, 249 F. Supp. 2d 357, 378-80 (S.D.N.Y. 2003); *United States v. Gleneagles Inv. Co.*, 565 F. Supp. at 578, *aff'd sub nom., United States v. Tabor Court Realty Corp.*, 803 F.2d 1288 (3d Cir. 1986), *cert. denied* 483 U.S. 1005 (1987); 12 Pa C.S. § 5102, Committee Comment (1993).

Whether the claim is one for actual or constructive fraudulent transfers, the plaintiff has the burden of proving the debtor's insolvency, either as part of her *prima facie* case or to establish a "badge of fraud". *Constructora Maza, Inc. v. Banco de Ponce*, 616 F.2d 573, 577 (1st Cir. 1980); *United States v. Hansel*, 999 F. Supp. 694, 699 (N.D.N.Y 1998) (party challenging conveyance has burden of proving insolvency); *In re Bayou*, 439 at B.R. at 330.

Good insolvency experts can be costly, but are critical, especially in cases involving constructive fraud, where proof of insolvency is a required element of the plaintiff's *primafacie* case. Whether you represent a plaintiff or a defendant, hire and use an insolvency expert early and wisely. Preliminary insolvency opinions conducted by non-testifying consulting experts performed early in the case may be useful and cost effective. In federal practice, facts known and opinions held by an expert who has been retained or specifically employed in anticipation of litigation or to prepare for trial and who is not expected to be called as a witness, ordinarily are not discoverable, but can become discoverable "on a showing of exceptional circumstances under which it is impracticable for the party to obtain facts or opinions on the same subject by other means", an unlikely circumstance in most cases. Fed. R. Civ. P. 26 (b)(4)(D). In state court practice, local rules should be consulted on the issue of discovery from testifying and non-testifying experts.

# 8.

## Tracing the property transferred

To identify and recover the transferred property (or its corresponding value in money) the plaintiff has the burden of tracing the movement of the property from the debtor to the initial transferee and to all subsequent transferees.[13] *In re International Administrative Services, Inc.*, 408 F.3d at 696-97, 702, 708 (noting that "the [t]rustee hired a forensic

---

[13]Under the Bankruptcy Code, the first recipient of fraudulently transferred property is referred to as the "initial transferee" and any subsequent transferees of the property are referred to as the "immediate or mediate transferee of such initial transferee". 11 U.S.C. § 550(a). The UFTA uses the term "subsequent transferee" for these latter two categories of transferees. 6 Del. C. § 1308(b); Cal. Civ. Code § 3439.08(b); 12 Pa.C.S. § 5108(b). Where the initial transfer has been avoided, the Bankruptcy Code grants the plaintiff an additional year to bring an action to recover the transferred property from an immediate or mediate transferee or until the bankruptcy case is closed or dismissed, whichever is earlier. 11 U.S.C. § 550(f). Because the plaintiff must always identify and avoid the transfer to the initial transferee to recover, identification of a particular party as the "initial transferee" can be critical to the plaintiff's case. *In re International Administrative Services, Inc.*, 408 F.3d at 704-06.

accountant to assist in piercing through the jigsaw puzzle of transfers" and describing "a tangled and complex web of multi-step international transactions". "[T]he plaintiff has the burden of tracing funds it claims are property of the estate".); *First Federal of Michigan v. Barrow*, 878 F.2d 912 (6th Cir. 1989)(tracing was required to impose a constructive trust in a bankruptcy case involving commingled funds).

This means that the plaintiff must identify and avoid the initial transfer of the debtor's property and then trace all movements of that property to subsequent transferees and seek to recover the property from them. *In re Administrative Services, Inc.*, 408 F.3d at 705-09. The Bankruptcy Code and state fraudulent transfer statutes provide the plaintiff with this remedy to prevent situations in which assets are made non-recoverable simply by being moved from one entity to the next by clever or deceitful persons. *Id.* at 706-08.

Tracing asset movements, especially when a large number of cash transfers have been made over a long time period, can be complex, especially in egregious cases. *Id.* at 706 ("Money changed multiple hands, twenty-three entities filtered IAS funds away from creditors"). In such situations, parties are well advised to engage experienced forensic accountants early in the case to perform the required tracing, which can be tedious and time consuming. *Id.* at 705-09; *see* also *James D. Lyon, Chapter 7 Trustee v. Ferguson, et al. (In re ClassicStar Mare Lease Litigation)*, Civil Action No. 09-215-JMH, Docket No. 40 at 55-64 (E.D. Ky. 2009); *Cunningham v. Brown, et al.*, 265 U.S. at 11 ("But to succeed they [the plaintiffs] must trace the money, and therein they have failed").

While accounting records can vary from case to case and business to business, there are some general categories of documents typically used by forensic accountants to trace transfers, notably transfers of cash. Subject to consultation with accounting and forensic experts in a given case, below are some examples of the types of accounting documents that may be useful in performing cash tracing:

- General ledger
- Journal entries
- Bank account statements
- Bank account reconciliations
- Correspondence between bank and debtor's accounting personnel or other managers
- Checkbook register
- Bank account deposit documents
- Bank detail reports
- Disbursement request forms
- Debtor's cash control records
- Wire transfer requests and logs
- Income tax returns
- Tax reporting records

Other documents may, of course, be useful depending upon the type of property at issue. Tracing the movement of real estate or intellectual property, for example, obviously will involve different documents than the tracing of cash.

# 9.

## Bankruptcy Code vs. state law

As previously noted, the two general sources of fraudulent transfer law that come into play for private litigants are the fraudulent transfer provisions of the Bankruptcy Code and state fraudulent transfer statutes. 11 U.S.C. §§ 544(b)(1), 548, 550; *e.g.* 6 Del. C. § 1301, *et seq.*; Cal. Civ. Code § 3439.01, *et seq.*; 12 Pa. C.S. § 5101, *et seq.;* Kentucky Revised Statutes ("KRS") § 378.010; New York Debtor and Creditor Law §§ 270-281. The fraudulent transfer provisions used solely in bankruptcy cases set forth in §§ 548 and 550 of the Bankruptcy Code, like their state law counterparts, include provisions for the avoidance and recovery of intentional and constructive fraudulent transfers.[14]

---

[14] Recognizing the similarity between the fraudulent transfer provisions of the Bankruptcy Code and state fraudulent transfer statutes, courts will

State fraudulent transfer statutes can be used in non-bankruptcy cases filed in state or federal courts and also in bankruptcy cases pursuant to the trustee's so-called "strong-arm" powers contained in § 544 of the Bankruptcy Code. State fraudulent transfer statutes are generally of three types: (1) those that follow UFTA; (2) those that follow the older UFCA; and (3) those that appear to follow neither. *E.g.*, 6 Del. C. § 1301, *et seq.* (follows UFTA); Cal. Civ. Code § 3439.01, *et seq.* (follows UFTA); 12 Pa. C.S. § 5101, *et seq.* (follows UFTA); New York Debtor and Creditor Law, §§ 270-281 (follows UFCA); KRS §§ 378.010, .020, .030 (appears to follow neither UFTA nor UFCA strictly).

One of the principal differences between state fraudulent transfer statutes and the fraudulent transfer provisions in the Bankruptcy Code, is the length of time over which transfers or obligations can be avoided - the length of the so-

---

often draw upon cases interpreting both laws when rendering decisions in fraudulent transfer litigation. *Hayes v. Palm Seedlings Partners-A (In re Agricultural Research and Technology Group, Inc.)*, 916 F.2d 528, 537 (9th Cir. 1990); *Donell v. Kowell*, 533 F.3d 762, 767 (9th Cir. 2008). *See also* Cal. Civ. Code § 3439.11 ("This chapter shall be applied and construed to effectuate its general purpose to make uniform the law with respect to the subject of this chapter among states enacting it"). *Harbinger Capital Partners Master Fund I, Ltd. v. Granite Broadcasting Corp., et al.*, 906 A. 2d 218, 223 (Del. Ch. 2006)(noting the absence of differences in results under various uniform fraudulent transfer laws); *Charys Liquidating Trust, etc. v. McMahan Securities Co., L.P. (In re Charys Holding Company, Inc.)*, 443 B.R. 628, 636 (Bankr. D. Del. 2010) (noting similarities between the UFTA, the UFCA and § 548 of the Bankruptcy Code).

called "reach back" or "look back" period. Section 548 of the Bankruptcy Code (since its amendment in 2005), allows for the avoidance of fraudulent transfers made up to two years before the date of the filing of debtor's bankruptcy petition, while UFTA and most state fraudulent transfer statutes that follow UFTA, contain a four-year reach back period. For cases involving intentional fraud, states that follow the UFTA often also provide a reach back period that extends to "within one year after the transfer or obligation could reasonably have been discovered by the claimant", effectively permitting a plaintiff to reach back farther than four years. 11 U.S.C. § 548(a)(1) (extended the pre-2005 one-year reach back period to two years and added avoidance of payments to insiders under employment contracts under certain circumstances), HR Rep. No. 31, 109th Cong., 1st Sess. 1402 (2005); 6 Del. C. § 1309; Cal. Civ. Code § 3439.09; 12Pa. C.S. § 5109.

There are some notable variations among fraudulent transfer statutes to the usual four-year reach back period, such as the Kentucky fraudulent transfer statute, which applies a five-year statute of limitations, and the New York Debtor and Creditor Law, which applies a six-year statute of limitations. *Pergrem v. Smith*, 255 S.W.2d 42, 43-44 (Ky. 1953); *Gillardi v. Henry*, 113 S.W.2d 1158, 1162 (Ky. 1938)(Kentucky fraudulent transfers are subject to a five-year statute of limitations); KRS §§ 378.010, 413.130; NY CLS CPLR § 213; *Childs v. Brandon*, 90 A. D. 2d 983, 984 (N.Y. App. Div. 4th Dep't 1982)("the New York Statute of Limitations for constructive fraud is six years and runs from the commission of the wrong"). State law should be consulted on this issue.[15]

Another significant difference that applies to claims for constructive fraudulent transfers under the New York Debtor and Creditor Law, is the requirement that the plaintiff prove the absence of good faith by the defendant as part of its proof of lack of "fair consideration" received by the debtor in exchange for the transfer or obligation. New York Debtor and Creditor Law at § 272; *In re Sharp International Corp.*, 403 F.3d at 53-55 ("[F]air consideration requires that the exchange not only be for equivalent value, but also that the conveyance be made in good faith") *citingHB Leasing Corp. v. Frank*, 48 F.3d at 633-36 ("the statutory requirement of 'good faith' is satisfied if the transferee acted without

---

[15] One authority has noted that "[s]tatutes of limitations applicable to the avoidance of fraudulent transfers and obligations vary widely from state to state and are frequently subject to uncertainties in their application." 12 Pa. C.S. § 5109, Committee Comment (1993). Adoption of the UFTA and its provision applying a stated four-year reach back period, was intended to "mitigate the uncertainty and diversity that have characterized the decisions applying statutes of limitations to actions to [sic] fraudulent transfers and obligations". *Id.*

either actual or constructive knowledge of any fraudulent scheme").

# 10.

**Reach back and limitations periods**

In addition to reach-back periods used to determine the time frame over which transfers and obligations can be avoided, the Bankruptcy Code and state law also impose limitations periods by which a fraudulent transfer claim must be prosecuted. As discussed in more detail below, these state and federal time periods may or may not be subject to extension by the doctrine of equitable tolling. Counsel should be aware of the potential interplay between reach back periods, statutes of limitations and the doctrine of equitable tolling.

Section 548(a)(1) of the Bankruptcy Code permits the plaintiff to recover transfers or obligations incurred by the debtor up to two years before the date of the filing of the debtor's bankruptcy petition. Thus, under this two-year reach back period, if the debtor filed for bankruptcy on July 1, 2013, the plaintiff could seek to avoid transfers or obligations of the debtor that occurred on or after July 1, 2011, but no later than June 30, 2013. Most state fraudulent transfer statutes provide for a four-year reach back period or longer, meaning that if a fraudulent transfer action were filed in a non-bankruptcy case on July 1, 2013, the plaintiff could seek to avoid transfers or obligations that occurred on or after July 1, 2009, but no later than June 30, 2013. In fraudulent transfer cases brought under state law pursuant to the trustee's "strong arm" powers in 11 U.S.C. § 544, the four-year reach back period (or longer, depending upon state law) would run from four years before the date of the filing of the debtor's bankruptcy petition.

Can either the two-year reach back period in the Bankruptcy Code or the four-year (or longer) reach back period under state law, be extended by equitable tolling?

The two-year reach back period in § 548(a)(1) of the Bankruptcy Code generally is not subject to equitable tolling, although there is some authority providing that it can be extended under limited circumstances.[16]

---

[16]The author currently is aware of only one decision in which a court recognized that the two-year reach back period in § 548(a)(1) of the Bankruptcy Code can be extended by equitable tolling. See *Official Committee of Unsecured Creditors v. Pardee (In re Stanwich Financial Services Corp.),* 291 B.R. 25, 28 (Bankr. D. Conn. 2003)("*Stanwich*"). In *Stanwich,* the court stated that extending the two-year reach back period in § 548(a)(1) of the Bankruptcy Code can be accomplished only upon a

State law reach back periods may be subject to equitable tolling under state law. State fraudulent transfer statutes that follow the UFTA generally contain a provision allowing for a one-year extension of the four-year reach back period "after the transfer or obligation was or could reasonably have been discovered by the claimant" for cases involving intentional fraudulent transfers, but not for cases involving constructive fraudulent transfers. *E.g.*, 6 Del. C. § 1309; Cal. Civ. Code § 3439.09; 12 Pa.C.S. § 5109. The plaintiff has the burden of proving equitable tolling. *Holmberg v. Armbrecht*, 327 U.S. 392, 397 (1946); *End of the Road Trust, ex rel. Freuhauf Trailer Corp. v. Terex Corp. (In re Freuhauf Trailer Corporation)*, 250 B.R. 168, 193 (D. Del. 2000); *In re International Administrative Services, Inc.*, 408 F.3d at 701; *Akande v. Transamerica Airlines, Inc. (In re Transamerica Airlines, Inc.)*, 2006 Del. Ch. LEXIS 47 at *12-*17 (Del, Ch. 2006).

---

showing of "wrongful concealment", which requires that the plaintiff show (1) wrongful concealment by the defendant, (2) which prevented the plaintiff's discovery of the nature of the claim within the limitations period, and (3) due diligence in pursuing discovery of the claim. *Id.* This is a heavy burden. *Cf. Industrial Enterprises of America, Inc. v. Burtis, et al. (In re Pitt Penn Holding Co.)*, 2012 Bankr. LEXIS 325 at *7-*14 (Bankr. D. Del. 2012) (two-year reach back period in § 548 of the Bankruptcy Code is not a statute of limitations, but a substantive element of the trustee's claim and is not subject to equitable tolling, expressly rejecting *Stanwich*).

Therefore, any party to a fraudulent transfer action, whether a plaintiff or a defendant, should carefully identify all applicable reach back periods and, in light of the facts presented and state law that may apply, determine whether those periods can be extended by equitable tolling based on provisions in the statute or case law, which could result in more transfers or obligations being subject to avoidance.

There are also statute of limitations in the Bankruptcy Code that come into play, whether a fraudulent transfer claim is brought under § 548 of the Bankruptcy Code, or under state fraudulent transfer law pursuant to the trustee's strong arm powers in 11 U.S.C. in § 544. Section 546(a) of the Bankruptcy Code provides that, assuming an applicable state law statute of limitations has not expired before the filing of the debtor's bankruptcy petition, then the trustee, the debtor-in-possession or other authorized estate representative, is granted an additional two years from the date of the filing of the debtor's bankruptcy petition (or one year after the appointment or election of a trustee, or until the bankruptcy case is closed, whichever is later), to bring fraudulent transfer claims under 11 U.S.C. § 548 or state law. 11 U.S.C. § 546(a).[17] The purpose of this provision is to provide the

---

[17]Similarly, § 108(a) of the Bankruptcy Code provides for a two-year extension period to bring claims belonging to the debtor's estate that are governed by time periods under state law or by time periods contained in

estate representative, who is typically an after-the-fact outsider with no personal knowledge of the facts, sufficient time to investigate and bring claims for the benefit of the debtor's estate and its creditors. *In re APF Co.*, 274 B.R. at 638; *In re Global Link Liquidating Trust, etc.*, 327 B.R. at 717. The time periods in § 546(e) are subject to equitable tolling. *In re International Administrative Services, Inc.*, 408 F.3d. at 699-702; *In re Fruehauf Trailer Corporation, et al.*, 250 B.R. at 193.

Therefore, prospective defendants facing exposure to fraudulent transfer claims on the date of the debtor's bankruptcy filing, will not be free of that exposure for at least two more years. Estate representatives such as trustees, debtors-in-possession, court-appointed official committees or others with approval from the court to bring fraudulent transfer claims, should investigate all potential fraudulent transfer claims promptly and allow sufficient time to draft and file an appropriate complaint before the expiration of the time periods in 11 U.S. C. § 546(a).

---

court orders entered in non-bankruptcy proceedings, if those time periods have not expired as of the date of the filing of the debtor's bankruptcy petition. 11 U.S.C. § 108(a).

# 11.

**Who can sue to recover fraudulent transfers?**

In a case under chapter 11 of the Bankruptcy Code, the plaintiff in a fraudulent transfer case can be either the debtor-in-possession, a chapter 11 trustee, a court-appointed receiver, or the trustee of a liquidating trust formed as part of a confirmed chapter 11 plan of reorganization or liquidation. *See* 11 U.S.C. § 1107; *Donell v. Kowell*, 533 F.3d 762 (receiver); *In re PWS Holding Corporation, et al.*, 303 F.3d at 314 (trustee, debtor-in-possession); *In re Appleseed's Intermediate Holdings LLC, et al.*, Chapter 11, Case No. 11-10160-KG, Joint Plan of Reorganization, etc., Docket No. 638 (Bankr. D. Del. 2011)(liquidating trust); *In re Global Link Telecom Corporation, et al.*, 327 B.R. at 714 (liquidating trust).

Official committees appointed in chapter 11 cases may also be plaintiffs in fraudulent transfer cases if granted such authority by the court. *The Official Committee of Unsecured Creditors of Cybergenics Corporation, et al. v. Chinery, et al. (In re Cybergenics Corporation)*, 330 F.3d 548, 566 (3d Cir. 2003); *Official Committee of Unsecured Creditors v. R.F. Lafferty & Co., Inc., et al.*, 267 F.2d 340, 344 (3d Cir. 2001).

In a chapter 7 case, the plaintiff in a fraudulent transfer action is the chapter 7 trustee.[18]*See* 11 U.S.C. §§ 704, 1106; *e.g., James D. Lyon, Chapter 7 Trustee of ClassicStar, LLC v. Ferguson, et al. (In re ClassicStar Mare Lease Litigation)*, Civil Action No. 09-215-JMH, Docket No. 40 (E.D. Ky. 2009).

Because a fraudulent transfer claim becomes property of the debtor's estate upon a bankruptcy filing (*see* discussion below), only in rare cases will an individual creditor have standing to bring a fraudulent transfer claim in a bankruptcy case. *National Tax Credit Partners, L.P. v. Havlik*, 20 F. 3d 705, 708-09 (7th Cir. 1994). To do so, the creditor

---

[18] While not the subject of this book, a debtor in a case under chapter 13 of the Bankruptcy Code may have the right to file an action to avoid a fraudulent transfer to the extent the debtor could have claimed an exemption for the property transferred and the trustee does not seek to avoid the transfer of the exempt property. 11 U.S.C. § 522(h); *In re Coleman*, 21 B.R. at 835.

must first make demand on the trustee or debtor-in-possession, who must refuse to bring the fraudulent transfer claim, and then the bankruptcy court must grant the creditor authority to pursue the claim. *Hall v. Walter (In re Hall)*, 139 F.3d 911, *2-*4 (10th Cir. 1998) (un-published opinion); *Best Manufacturing v. White Plains Coat and Apron Co. (In re Daniele Landries, Inc.)*, 40 B.R. 404, 408 (Bankr. S.D.N.Y. 1984); *Board of Teamsters Local 863 Pension Fund v. Foodtown, Inc.*, 296 F.3d 164, 169 (3d Cir. 2002).

Under all such scenarios, the goal of the plaintiff in any fraudulent transfer case is to recover assets for the debtor's estate for the ultimate benefit of the debtor's unsecured creditors. 11 U.S.C. § 704; *Wellman v. Wellman*, 933 F.2d 215, 218 (4th Cir. 1991) *cert. denied*, 502 U.S. 925 (1991) (there must be a benefit to creditors); *In re PWS Holding Corp.*, 303 F.3d at 314 (individual creditor could not bring fraudulent transfer claim); *e.g.,James D. Lyon, Chapter 7 Trustee of ClassicStar LLC v. Ferguson, et al. (In re ClassicStar Mare Lease Litigation)*, Civil Action No. 09-215-JMH, Docket No. 40 (E.D. Ky. 2009) (fraudulent transfer claims brought by chapter 7 trustee).

In a non-bankruptcy case, the plaintiff in a fraudulent transfer action will typically be an unsecured creditor of the debtor/transferor, as defined by the controlling state fraudulent transfer statute. *E.g.*, 6 Del. C. §§ 1301(3), (4), 1304(a), 1305, 1307; *Richards v. Jones*, 142 A. 832, 833 (Del. 1928) (one whose claim is in tort is a creditor); Cal. Civ. Code §§ 3439.01(c), 3439.04(a), 3439.05; 12 Pa. C.S. §§ 5101, 5104, 5105; *In re Bayou Group, LLC, et al.*, 439 B.R. at 303.

Receivers have also been granted standing to bring fraudulent transfer claims under state law, but only when the entity in receivership is a creditor of the debtor/transferor. *Friedman v. Wahrsager*, 848 F. Supp. 278, 289 (E.D.N.Y. 2012).

The right of a general unsecured creditor of a debtor to bring a state law fraudulent transfer claim passes, by operation of law, to the debtor-in-possession, trustee or other court-approved estate representative, upon the filing of the debtor/transferor's bankruptcy petition. *Hassett v. McColley (In re O.P.M. Leasing Services, Inc., et al.)*, 28 B.R. 740, 759 (Bankr. S.D.N.Y. 1983); *Belfance v. Bushey (In re Bushey)*, 210 B.R. 95, 100 (6th Cir. B.A.P. 1997); 11 U.S.C. § 544(b)(1). As previously noted, the power of the debtor-in-possession, trustee or other court-approved plaintiff to "step into the shoes" of a creditor to bring a fraudulent transfer claim under state law, is set forth in § 544 of the Bankruptcy Code and is referred to as the "strong arm power." 11 U.S.C. § 544(b); *National Labor Relations Board v. Arsham*, 873

F.3d at 887; *In re Independence Clearing House Company*, 77 B.R. at 863 n. 30; *see e.g.James D. Lyon, Chapter 7 Trustee of ClassicStar, LLC v. Ferguson, et al.* (*In re ClassicStar Mare Lease Litigation*), Civil Action No. 09-215-JMH, Docket No. 40 (E.D. Ky. 2009); *In re National Audit Defense Network*, 367 B.R. at 213 n. 5. Otherwise, a trustee lacks authority to bring a claim directly on behalf of a debtor's creditors. *Caplin v. Marine Midland Trust Co.*, 406 U.S. 416, 428-34 (1972).

## 12.

**Who can be sued to recover fraudulent transfers?**

The likely defendants in a fraudulent transfer case can vary, but generally speaking are, in addition to the first (initial) transferee who received the property transferred, any party that received or benefitted from the transfer or obligation, or any subsequent transferees of such persons. 11 U.S.C. § 550(a); 6 Del. C. § 1308(b); Cal. Civ. Code § 3439.08(b); 12 Pa. C.S. § 5108(b).[19] Defendants in a fraudulent transfer action may include, for example, the debtor's insiders, such as current or former officers, directors or affil-

---

[19]As previously noted in footnote 13 *supra*, the Bankruptcy Code defines subsequent transferees as the "immediate or mediate transferee of such initial transferee." 11 U.S.C. § 550 (a). State fraudulent transfer statutes that follow UFTA, typically use the term "subsequent transferee" to describe all transferees other than the initial transferee. *E.g.*,6 Del. C. § 1308(b)(2); Cal. Civ. C. § 3439.8 (b)(2); 12 Pa.C.S. § 5108(b)(2).

iates[20] and/or non-insiders of the debtor that received or benefitted from the transfers or obligation. *E.g., James D. Lyon, Chapter 7 Trustee of ClassicStar, LLC v. Ferguson, et al.*(*In re ClassicStar Mare Lease Litigation*), Civil Action No. 09-215-JMH, Docket No. 40 (E.D. Ky. 2009)(debtor's former officers, affiliates and other insiders sued for the recovery of fraudulent transfers); 11 U.S.C. § 550(a); *In re International Administrative Services, Inc.*, 408 F.3d at 703-09 (the debtor's money was transferred around the globe through two dozen separate entities); *In re National Audit Defense Network*, 367 B.R. at 212 (debtor's officers sued for receipt of fraudulent transfers).

Payments by the debtor on a legitimate outstanding debt (referred to as an "antecedent" debt) or transfers to a transferee who takes for value in good faith and without knowledge that the transfer or obligation is avoidable, will generally not be recoverable as fraudulent transfers. *See*11

---

[20] "Insiders" of the debtor include corporate affiliates, officers, directors and controlling persons of the debtor, among others. *Seee.g.*11 U.S.C. § 101(31); 6 Del. C. § 1301(7), Annotated Laws of Massachusetts, General Law ch. 109A, § 2 (2010). The Bankruptcy Code and state fraudulent transfer statutes also contain provisions relating to the recovery of fraudulent transfers from insiders of the debtor and provisions that grant a lien to an initial transferee from whom the plaintiff may recover a fraudulent transfer if such initial transferee gave value and acted in good faith. 11 U.S.C. §§ 548(c), 550(e); 6 Del. C. § 1308(d); Cal. Civ. Code § 3439-08(d); 12 Pa. C. S. § 5108(d); *TSIC, Inc., etc. v. Thalheimer* (*In re TSIC, Inc.*), 428 B.R. 103, 109 (Bankr. D. Del. 2010); *In re Trans Texas Gas Corp.*, 597 F.3d at 305-06.

U.S.C. §§ 548(d)(2)(A), 550(b); *In re Carrozzella & Richardson*, 286 B.R. at 489; 6 Del. C. § 1308(b)(2); Cal. Civ. Code § 3439.08(b)(2) (2011); 12 Pa. C.C. § 5108(b)(2).

In all cases, the first transfer (often referred to as the initial transfer) *must* be avoided before any recovery can be had against any subsequent transferees, although in most courts the plaintiff need not go through the exercise of naming the initial transferee as a defendant if no recovery is sought from him. *See In re International Administrative Services Inc.*, 408 F.3d at 703-08 (once the plaintiff avoids the transfer to the initial transferee, he can then skip over the initial transferee and recover from those next in line who received the property).

## 13.

**How much money can be recovered?**

Under the Bankruptcy Code, the damages recoverable by a successful plaintiff in a fraudulent transfer action are the return of the property transferred or payment to the plaintiff of the property's value in money. 11 U.S.C. § 550(a). This is consistent with the broad remedial provisions in most state fraudulent transfer statutes. In addition, state statutes that follow the UFTA grant the plaintiff the right to seek an attachment or other provisional remedies, injunctions, the appointment of a receiver and "[a]ny relief the circumstances may require". 6 Del. C. §§ 1307(a)(1), 1308(b); Cal. Civ. Code; §§ 3439.07(a)(1), 3439.08 (b); 12 Pa. C.S. §§ 5107(a)(1), 5108(b). Attorney's fees and punitive damages may also be available for cases involving intentional fraudulent transfers. *E.g.*, New York Debtor and Creditor Law §

276-a; *Youngstown Osteopathic Hospital Association v. Pathways Center for Geriatric Psychiatry, Inc., et al.(In re Youngstown Osteopathic Hospital Association)*, 280 B.R. 400, 410 (Bankr. N.D. Oh. 2002).

To provide a hypothetical: if it is determined at trial that the debtor fraudulently transferred $3.5 million in cash to its parent company (the initial transferee) and the $3.5 million was then further transferred by the parent company to an individual insider of the debtor, then (assuming both transferees were named as defendants in the case) a monetary judgment would be entered for $3.5 million against the parent company (the initial transferee) and the individual insider (the subsequent transferee), which would allow the plaintiff to collect on the judgment from either defendant for the amounts they actually received until the entire $3.5 million is recovered. 11 U.S.C. § 550(a); 11 U.S.C. § 550(d)("The trustee is entitled to only a single satisfaction under subsection (a) of this section"); 6 Del. C. § 1308(b); Cal. Civ. Code § 3439.08(b); 12 Pa.C.S. § 5108(b). A victorious plaintiff would also be permitted to seek pre and post judgment interest on the $3.5 million judgment, similar to judgments in other civil cases. *E.g., In re International Administrative Services, Inc.*, 408 F.3d at 709-10; *James D. Lyon v. Neil Baker (In re ClassicStar, LLC)*, Adv. No. 09-5155, Docket

Nos. 117, 124 (Bankr. E.D. Ky. 2011) (unpublished); *In re Slatkin*, 525 F.3d at 820 (court has discretion to award prejudgment interest on summary judgment in a fraudulent transfer case).

Once the fraudulent transfer judgment is final, it is subject to traditional execution rules that apply to all civil judgments. *Id.*; Fed. R. Bankr. P. 7069 (incorporates Fed. R. Civ. P. 69, Execution., into adversary proceedings in bankruptcy cases).

# 14.

### Writing the complaint

If the fraudulent transfer action is filed in federal court, then federal rules of pleading set forth in the Federal Rules of Civil Procedure, as interpreted by federal case law, apply. Fed. R. Civ. P. 8, 9; *Mervyn's Holdings, LLC v. Lubert-Adler Group IV, LLC (In re Mervyn's Holdings, LLC)*, 426 B.R. 488, 495 (Bankr. D. Del. 2010); *Bell Atlantic Corp. v. Twombly*, 550 U.S. 544, 562 (2007); *Ashcroft v. Iqbal*, 129 S. Ct. 1937, 1949 (2009); Fed R. Bankr. P. 7008 (applying and adding to, Fed. R. Civ. P. 8 for adversary proceedings in bankruptcy cases); Fed. R. Bankr. P. 7009 (incorporating Fed. R. Civ. P. 9 into bankruptcy matters).

Thus, a fraudulent transfer complaint, like complaints in other federal civil actions, "must contain either direct or inferential allegations respecting all the material elements necessary to sustain recovery under some viable legal theory." *Twombly*, 550 U.S. at 562. "To prevent dismissal all civil complaints must now set out 'sufficient factual matter' to show that the claim is facially plausible." *Ashcroft v. Iqbal*, 129 S. Ct. at 1949-50. A complaint need not contain detailed factual allegations, but "a plaintiff's obligation to provide the 'grounds' of his 'entitle[ment] to relief' requires more than labels and conclusions, and a formulaic recitation of the elements of a cause of action will not do... Factual allegations must be enough to raise a right to relief above the speculative level." *Twombly*, 550 U.S. at 555. "The relevant record consists of the complaint and any 'document integral to or explicitly relied on in the complaint.'" *U.S. Express Lines, Ltd. v. Higgins*, 281 F.3d 383, 388 (3d Cir. 2002). In fraudulent transfer actions filed in state court, state law pleading standards will apply. *See e.g.*, Pa. R. Civ. P. 1024 (averments or denial of fact in a pleading that are not of record must be verified); Del. Ch. Rule 3 (aa) (complaints shall be verified).

Despite the well-known differences between common law fraud, which focuses on compensating injured plaintiffs for misrepresentations of material fact made to them by the defendant, and fraudulent transfer law, which focuses on preserving the debtor's assets for the benefit of the debtor's unsecured creditors, the particularity requirement of Fed. R. Civ. P. 9(b) has nevertheless been held to apply to complaints alleging intentional fraudulent transfers.[21] *Feldman v. Chase Home Finance (In re Image Masters, Inc.)*, 421 B.R. 164, 184-185 (Bankr. E.D. Pa. 2009); *Wahoski v. Classic Packaging Co. (In re Pillowtex Corporation)*, 427 B.R. 301, 310 (Bankr. D. Del. 2010); *In re Global Link TelecomCorporation*, 327 B.R. at 717-18 (compares the pleading of common law fraud to fraudulent transfers and notes the more liberal pleading rule for fraudulent transfer claims asserted by trustees in bankruptcy cases).

Although some cases have concluded that the particularity requirement of Fed. R. Civ. P. 9(b) also applies to claims for constructive fraudulent transfers, the majority view appears to be that it does not. *OHC Liquidating Trust v. Nucor Corp. (In re Oakwood Homes Corp.)*, 325 B.R. 696, 698 (Bankr. D. Del. 2005); *In re Charys Holding Company, Inc.*, 443 B.R. at 632 n.2. *In re Global Link Telecom Corp.*, 327 B.R. at 717-18 ("[A] claim of constructive fraud need not allege the common variety of deceit, misrepresentation or fraud in the inducement").

Taking the Rule 9 particularity requirement into account, from the plaintiff's perspective, the more detail and

---

[21] Fed. R. Civ. P. 9 applies in adversary proceedings in bankruptcy cases. *See* Fed. R. Bankr. P. 7009.

specificity that can be alleged in a fraudulent transfer complaint, whether the claims are based on intentional or constructive fraud, the more likely the complaint will be to survive a motion to dismiss. Setting forth the following allegations in the complaint should help a fraudulent transfer complaint survive dismissal at the pleading stage: (i) clear identification of the debtor and a description of the debtor's business and economic condition at the time of the transfer or obligation; (ii) a thorough description of the property transferred or the obligation incurred; (iii) a clear description of the debtor's interest in the property transferred; (iv) the dates of, method of, and description of, the transfer or obligation, including step-by-step results of all tracing from the debtor to the initial transferee and to any subsequent transferees; (v) the identity by name and role of each initial transferee, each subsequent transferee and each beneficiary of the transfer or obligation; (vi) a description of all value received by the debtor in exchange for the transfer or obligation, if any, or a clear statement that no or insufficient value was received by the debtor in exchange for the transfer or obligation and a description of the basis for that determination; (vii) any other facts relevant to show that the transferee did not provide reasonably equivalent value or fair consideration in good faith in exchange for the transfer or obligation;

(viii) a description of any relevant insider relationships; (ix) a description of the debtor's insolvency and financial condition at the time of the transfer or obligation, and/or as a result of the transfer or obligation, with assistance from a qualified expert, as needed; (x) in cases involving claims for intentional fraudulent transfers, a thorough recitation of all facts showing the presence of two or more badges of fraud; and (xi) a clear statement of all damages sought. *In re National Audit Defense Network*, 367 B.R. at 212-14 (description of debtor's business and role of defendants), 215 (description of Ponzi-type scheme), 219 (description of transfers), 219-20 (description of badges of fraud), 225 (description of reasonably equivalent value), 228 (alter ego); *In re International Administrative Services, Inc.*, 408 F.3d at 702 (forensic accountant assisted "in piecing together a jigsaw puzzle of transfers"); *In re Bayou Group, LLC, et al.*, 439 B.R. at 291-94 (debtor's business, scheme, cover up, collapse and transfers).

Reviewing other well-pleaded fraudulent transfer complaints from public dockets is helpful. Below are several examples available through the federal court website Pacer (www.pacer.gov):

- *James D. Lyon v. Ferguson, et al. (In re ClassicStar Mare Lease Litigation)*, Civil Action

No. 09-215-JMK, Docket No. 40 (E.D. Ky. 2009)

- *Official Committee of Unsecured Creditors of Tousa, Inc., et al. v. Citigroup North America, Inc., et al. (In re Tousa, Inc., et al.)*, Adversary No. 08-01435-JKO-A, Docket No. 1 (Bankr. S.D. Fla. 2008)

- *Bayou Accredited Fund, LLC, et al. v. Redwood Growth Partners LLC, et al. (In re Bayou Group, LLC, et al.)*, Adversary No. 06-08318-RDD, Docket No. 1 (Bankr. S.D.N.Y. 2006).

- *Mervyn's LLC v. Lubert-Adler Group IV, et al. (In re Mervyn's Holdings LLC, et al.)*, Adversary No. 08-51402-KG, Docket No. 7 (Bankr. D. Del. 2008).

# 15.

## Defending

Defending against a fraudulent transfer claim will usually involve three general areas, as may be required by the circumstances: (1) attacking the plaintiff's *prima facie* case; (2) asserting the "good faith" defense; and/or (3) in bankruptcy cases, attacking the plaintiff's standing to sue under state law pursuant to the strong arm power. 11 U.S.C. §§ 544, 548, 550; 6 Del. C. § 1308 (b)(2); Cal. Civ. Code § 3439.08; 12 Pa. C. S. § 5108(a); New York Debtor and Creditor Law § 272 (good faith is a component of fair consideration). Other defenses, such as those listed in Fed R. Civ. P. 12(b) or available under state law that may be apply to a particular case, such as the statute of limitations, among others, can also be raised. *Diamond v. Friedman (In re Century City Doctors Hospital, LLC)*, 466 B.R. 1, 8 (Bankr. C.D. Cal.

2012). This chapter will focus on areas (1), (2) and (3) above, as they are unique to fraudulent transfer cases.

### a. Attacking the plaintiff's *prima facie* case

Attacking the plaintiff's *prima facie* case in a fraudulent transfer action typically involves showing one or more of the following:

(1) <u>The transfers or obligations occurred outside the fraudulent transfer reach back period</u>. A defendant should study all applicable reach back periods under federal and state law and challenge as untimely, all transfers or obligations that the plaintiff seeks to recover which fall outside the two-year, four-year or other applicable reach back period. The date of each transfer or obligation can be determined by applying the definition of "transfer" from the Bankruptcy Code, the UFTA or the UFCA, and then counting the days backwards from the bankruptcy filing date or complaint filing date, as the case may be, to the date the transfer or obligation occurred. 11 U.S.C. § 101(54); 6 Del. C. § 1301(12); Cal. Civ. Code § 3439.01(i); 12 Pa. C.S. § 5101(b)(3). A defendant should be prepared to argue against any assertion by the plaintiff that a reach back period should be extended by equitable tolling. *See* Chapter 9, Bankruptcy Code vs. state law and Chapter 10, Reach back and limitation periods *supra*.

(2) <u>The defendant is not a transferee</u>. In certain factual situations, a defendant may be able to prove that it was not a transferee of the debtor's property because the defendant did not have dominion and control over the property transferred and was a mere "conduit" or "financial intermediary" through which the debtor's property passed on its way to another party and therefore the defendant is not a "transferee" , beneficiary or obligee from which the plaintiff can recover. *See* Chapter 4, What is an "interest of the debtor in property"?, at 31 n.9, *supra*.

(3) <u>No debtor property was transferred</u>. Similar to the "dominion and control" and similar arguments noted in paragraph (2) *supra*, a defendant may be able to prove that because the debtor did not have an interest in the property transferred, the plaintiff cannot recover the transfer of that property to the defendant as a fraudulent transfer. *SeeIn re Plassein*, 366 B.R. at 325, *aff'd* at 388 B.R. 46 (D. Del. 2008) (no transfer of the debtor's property was alleged, subjecting the complaint to dismissal); *In re Computrex, Inc.*, 403 F.3d at 811-12 (pursuant to its contracts with its customer, which directed the debtor to pay over certain funds to third parties, the debtor had no dominion or control over the funds and therefore had no property interest in the funds and the trustee could not recover them); *Appalachian Oil Company, Inc.*

*v. The Virginian Travel Plaza, Inc. (In re Appalachian Oil Company, Inc.)*, 2011 WL 2565692 at *1, *3-*5 (Bankr. E.D. Tenn. 2011); *In re International Administrative Services, Inc.*, 408 at 705-08 (party that is a "mere conduit" of property does not hold an interest in that property); *In re Tousa, Inc.*, 444 B.R. at 647; *In re Finley Kumble, et al.*, 130 F.3d at 55-59 (defendant was a mere conduit). *In re Independent Clearing House Company*, 77 B.R. at 853-54 (rejecting argument that property obtained by fraud does not become property of the debtor's estate); *See* Chapter 4, What is an "interest of the debtor in property"? at 31 n.9 *supra*.

(4) <u>Insufficient "badges of fraud" are present</u>. In a case involving claims for intentional fraudulent transfers, a defendant may be able to show that because the plaintiff has proven the presence of only one or no badges of fraud, no inference of actual intent by the debtor to hinder, delay or defraud creditors can be made and therefore the transfers or obligations cannot be avoided. *In Re Fedders North America, Inc.*, 405 B.R. at 545; 6 Del. C. § 1304(b); 12 Pa. C. S. § 5104(b); Cal. Civ. Code § 3439.04(b); *Fleming Companies, Inc. v. Rich*, 978 F.Supp. at 1297-98. *See* Chapter 6, "Constructive vs. "intentional" fraudulent transfers at 41 n. 11, *supra*).

(5) <u>Reasonably equivalent value or fair consideration was received by the debtor</u>. In cases involving claims for constructive fraudulent transfers, a defendant may be able to prove that reasonably equivalent value, or fair consideration, was received by the debtor in exchange for the transfer or obligation and therefore the transfers or obligation cannot be avoided. The same argument can also be used to defeat attempts by the plaintiff to prove the presence of a badge of fraud based on the absence of reasonably equivalent value or fair consideration. *BFP v. Resolution Trust Corp.*, 511 U.S. at 548; *In re Fedders North America, Inc.*, 405 B.R. at 546; *VFB LLC v. Campbell Soup Co.*, 482 F.2d 624, 631 (3d Cir. 2007). Expert valuation evidence may be necessary to support this defense. Under the New York Debtor and Creditor Law, a plaintiff must also prove the absence of good faith by the transferee to show lack of fair consideration. *See* New York Debtor and Creditor Law § 272.

(6) <u>The debtor was not insolvent</u>. In a case involving claims for constructive fraudulent transfers with respect to present or future creditors, a defendant should consider attacking the plaintiff's *prima facie* case by proving that the debtor was not insolvent, did not have unreasonably small capital and/or could pay its debts as they came due, at the time of the transfer or obligation, or as a result of the trans-

fer or obligation. 11 U.S.C. § 548 (a)(1)(B); 6 Del. C. § 1304 (a)(2); Cal. Civ. Code §3439.04 (a)(2); 12 Pa. C.S. § 5104 (a)(2). This approach can also be used by a defendant in a case seeking to recover intentional fraudulent transfers in which the plaintiff attempted to rely on the debtor's alleged insolvency to show the presence of a badge of fraud. 6 Del. C. § 1304 (b)(9); Cal. Civ. Code § 3439.04 (b)(9); 12 Pa. C.S. § 5104 (b)(9); *In re TWA*, 134 F.3d at 193-98; *In re Bayou Group, LLC*, 439 B.R. at 331-336.

### b. Attacking the plaintiff's standing to sue

In cases asserting state law fraudulent transfer claims pursuant to the § 544(b) "strong arm" powers in the Bankruptcy Code, a defendant may wish to challenge the trustee's case by arguing that the trustee lacks standing to sue to recover a fraudulent transfer because he cannot satisfy the requirements of state fraudulent transfer law.

To assert a fraudulent transfer claim under state law pursuant to 11 U.S.C. § 544(b), the trustee must prove, as a threshold matter, that the transfer or obligation could have been avoided by an unsecured creditor of the debtor under non-bankruptcy law had the bankruptcy case not been filed, and further that at least one such unsecured creditor has a claim that is an allowed claim in the debtor's bankruptcy case pursuant to § 502 of the Bankruptcy Code. 11 U.S.C. §

544(b); *In re Century City Doctors Hospital, LLC*, 466 B.R. at 7-8; *National Labor Relations Board v. Arsham*, 873 F.2d at 887; *In re Bushey*, 210 B.R. at 100, *citingSender v.Simon*, 84 F.3d 1299, 1304 (10th Cir. 1996); *Harris v. National Investment Finance Company Inc. (In re Akin)*, 64 B.R. 510, 513 (Bankr. W.D. Ky. 1986); *In re Carrozzella & Richardson*, 286 B.R. at 483 n.3 ("The Bankruptcy Code provides two avenues for a trustee to recover fraudulent transfers made by the debtor. A trustee may bring a claim under either § 548 or § 544, which incorporates state non-bankruptcy law, which in most states is the Uniform Fraudulent Transfer Act ('UFTA') or the older Uniform Fraudulent Conveyance Act ('UFCA')").[22]

When attacking the plaintiff's standing under 11 U.S.C. § 544(b), a defendant may want to consider obtaining discovery of the debtor's unsecured creditors from near the time of the transfer or obligation and comparing that information to the debtor's bankruptcy schedules and to the proofs of claim on file in the debtor's bankruptcy case, to de-

---

[22] Although a trustee must ultimately prove the presence of an unsecured creditor by name to support standing under 11 U.S.C. § 544 (b), courts usually do not require the trustee to identify such a creditor by name in the complaint, although the complaint "must [still] set forth sufficient information to outline the elements of [the] claim or to permit inferences to be drawn that these elements exist." *Walker v. South Central Bell Tel. Co.*, 904 F.2d 275, 277 (5th Cir. 1990); *In re APF Co., et al.*, 274 B.R. at 639; *Askanase v. Fatjo*, 1993 WL 208682 at *4 (S.D. Tex. 1993).

termine whether an unsecured creditor with standing to sue under state law exists and whether such an unsecured creditor also has an allowed claim in the debtor's bankruptcy case. If handled effectively, this defense strategy could create difficulties for the trustee in some cases, possibly in cases in which substantial time has passed between the time of the transfer or obligation and the date of the debtor's bankruptcy filing, allowing the debtor's unsecured creditor body to realign such that the unsecured creditors who existed at the time of the transfer or obligation, are no longer creditors of the debtor at the time of the bankruptcy filing. This could force the trustee to rely solely on a "future" unsecured creditor to establish standing to sue under state law as opposed to a "present" creditor and thereby restrict the trustee's claim to the "future" creditor provisions of the state UFTA. *See* 6 Del. §§ 1304 (Transfers fraudulent as to present and future creditors), 1305 (Transfers fraudulent as to present creditors); Cal. Civ. Code §§ 3439.04, 3439.05; Pa. C.S. §§ 5104, 5105.

If appropriate, a defendant may also wish to develop objections to proofs of claim filed in the debtor's bankruptcy case by such "future" creditors to prevent their claims from becoming allowed.

c.   **The "good faith" defense**

After the plaintiff proves a *prima facie* case for intentional or constructive fraudulent transfers, a transferee may still be able to prevent the plaintiff from recovering by relying on the "good faith" defense in § 548(c) of the Bankruptcy Code, which states:

> a transferee...of such a transfer...that takes for value and in good faith...may retain any interest transferred...to the extent that such transferee...gave value to the debtor in exchange for such transfer or obligation.

11 U.S.C. § 548(c). Like other affirmative defenses, the defendant has the burden of proving that it took for value and in good faith. *Breeden v. L.I. Bridge Fund, LLC (In re Bennett Funding Corp.)*, 232 B.R. 565, 573 (Bankr. N.D.N.Y. 1999); *In re Agricultural Research and Technology Group, Inc.*, 916 F.2d at 536.

The Bankruptcy Code does not define "good faith" and there appears to be little agreement about exactly what it means. *In re Bayou Group, LLC*, 439 B.R. at 309. One authority has stated that good faith under § 548(c) is generally determined by asking the question of whether the transferee had information at the time of the transfer or obligation that put it on inquiry notice that the debtor was insolvent or that the transfers might be for a fraudulent purpose. *Id.* at 309.

Did the transferee know the debtor was insolvent or engaged in a fraud at the time of the transfer or obligation or was the transferee aware of facts from which a reasonable person should have known of the debtor's fraudulent intent and did the transferee then conduct a diligent investigation of the known facts? *Id.* at 309-23. This inquiry is case and fact-specific and "does not lend itself to the application of rigid or absolute rules." *Id.* at 311 n. 24, 317; s*ee also In re National Audit Defense Network*, 367 B.R. at 223-24.

The good faith defense in 11 U.S.C. § 550(b) also has the effect of barring the plaintiff from recovering a fraudulent transfer from a subsequent transferee of a good faith initial transferee, if the subsequent transferee gave value and acted in good faith. The "good faith" defense in § 550(b) of the Bankruptcy Code extends to any immediate or mediate good faith transferee of any immediate or mediate transferee (i.e., any subsequent transferee) who took for value and in good faith. 11 U.S.C. § 550(b); 6 Del. Corp. § 1308(b)(2); Cal. Civ. Code § 3439.08(b)(2); 12 P.a. C.S. § 5108(b); *In re Bayou Group, LLC*, 439 B.R. at 303-04; *In re Coleman*, 21 B.R. at 836 ("The initial transferee from the debtor is protected only if he takes in good faith for value without knowledge of the voidability of the transfer avoided. Any subsequent transferee of a transferee meeting this standard is protected if he took the property in good faith"). If a trustee recovers a fraudulent transfer from a good faith transferee pursuant to 11 U.S.C. § 550(a), that good faith transferee may retain a lien on the property equal to the cost of any improvements made to the property less any profit realized from the property, or for the increase in value to the property as a result of any improvements. 11 U.S.C. § 550(e).[23]

### d. A procedural point for bankruptcy cases – final orders and judgments

By statute, bankruptcy judges are granted the power to hear and render final orders and judgments in "all cases under title 11 and all core proceedings arising under title 11." 28 U.S.C. § 157(b)(1). In non-core proceedings that are otherwise related to a case under title 11, the bankruptcy judge shall "submit proposed findings of fact and conclusions of law to the district court." 28 U.S.C. § 157(c)(2). *SeeMichaelson v. Golden Gate Private Equity, Inc., et al.* (*In re Appleseed's Intermediate Holdings, Inc., et al.*), 2011 U.S. Dist. Lexis 144315 at *4 (D. Del. 2011).

Recognizing this core/non-core distinction in bankruptcy cases, the Federal Rules of Bankruptcy Procedure re-

---

[23] As noted, under New York Debtor and Creditor Law § 272, to prove the absence of "fair consideration" the plaintiff must plead and prove that the transferee did not give value in good faith, i.e., the plaintiff must prove the absence of good faith by the transferee. New York Debtor and Creditor Law § 272; *In re Bayou Group, LLC*, 439 B.R. at 303-04.

quire that pleadings filed in adversary proceedings must contain a statement by the pleading party whether the proceeding is core or non-core and whether the pleader does or does not consent to the entry of final orders or judgments by the bankruptcy judge.[24] Fed. R. Bankr. P. 7008(a), 7012(b). While fraudulent transfer claims are designated by statute as core proceedings, the Supreme Court of the United States has recently put into question the power of bankruptcy courts to decide and to enter final judgments and orders on any state law claim asserted by representatives of a debtor's bankruptcy estate, which would include, by definition, state law fraudulent transfer claims. 28 U.S.C. § 157(b)(2)(H); *Stern v. Marshall,* 131 S. Ct. 2594, 2611, 2617-18 (2011) ("*Stern*").

While *Stern* has generated substantial controversy and numerous court decisions interpreting its meaning, the full scope and impact of *Stern* is still not known. A reasonable approach in light of *Stern* would be for parties in fraudulent transfer litigation in bankruptcy cases to comply with Fed. R. Bankr. P. 7008(a) and 7012(b) by designating on their first pleading whether the matter is core or non-core

---

[24] Pleadings include: a complaint; an answer to a complaint; an answer to a counterclaim designated as a counterclaim; an answer to a crossclaim; a third-party complaint; an answer to a third-party complaint; and, if the court orders one, a reply to an answer. Fed. R. Civ. P. 7(a); Fed. R. Bankr. P. 7007.

and stating whether they do or do not consent to the entry of final orders and judgments by the bankruptcy judge.

If a party does not consent to the entry of final orders or judgments by the bankruptcy judge, the bankruptcy judge would then be limited to submitting proposed findings of fact and conclusions of law to the district court for *de novo* review. 28 U.S.C. § 157(c)(1). This procedure would result in a decision from the district court, thereby avoiding problems with *Stern* and would also eliminate a layer of appeal. 28 U.S.C. § 158(a); *Stern v. Marshall*, 131 S. Ct. at 2603 ("Parties may appeal final judgments of a bankruptcy court in core proceedings to the district court, which reviews them under traditional appellate standards"); Fed. R. Bankr. P. 8001, *et seq.*; *In re Appleseed's Intermediate Holdings, Inc., et al.*, 2011 U.S. Dist. LEXIS 144315 at *10 (noting the "round of appeals" to the district court that would be avoided if a state law fraudulent transfer case were first heard in the district court instead of the bankruptcy court). *See* American Bar Association, Section on Business Law, Report to the House Delegates, February 2013 (discussing *Stern* and supporting the position of the United States Bankruptcy Judges that bankruptcy courts, with the consent of the parties, should be permitted to hear, determine and enter final orders and judgments in non-core matters that they may not hear under

Article III of the Constitution of the United States, absent such consent); *Paloian v. American Express Co. (In re Canopy Financial, Inc.)*, 2011 WL 3911082, *2-*5 (D. N.D. Ill. 2011) (Interpreting *Stern* to permit bankruptcy courts to enter proposed findings of fact and conclusions of law on fraudulent transfer claims asserted under § 548 of the Bankruptcy Code and Illinois state law).

# 16.

### Ponzi scheme problems

Next we discuss the infamous "Ponzi" scheme cases and their "Black Swan"[25] impact on business and the law, notably on the law of fraudulent transfers, where, in a strange turn of events, the victims of the Ponzi scheme often end up being sued by the bankruptcy trustee to put back whatever money they were lucky enough to get out before the scheme collapsed. How can this happen?

To answer this question, a good place to begin is with an authoritative definition of a Ponzi scheme, such as the fol-

---

[25] A "Black Swan" event is defined in Wikipedia as one "that is a surprise to the observer, has a major effect and after the fact is often inappropriately rationalized with the benefit of hindsight". The development of Black Swan theory has been attributed to author Nassim Nicholas Taleb. *See*, Nassim Nicholas Taleb, The Black Swan, The Impact of the Highly Improbable (2d Ed. 2010).

lowing one from the United States Court of Appeals for the Ninth Circuit:

> A Ponzi scheme is a fraudulent arrangement in which an entity makes payments to investors from monies obtained from later investors rather than from any "profits" of the underlying business venture. The fraud consists of funneling proceeds received from new investors to previous investors in the guise of profits from the alleged business venture, thereby cultivating an illusion that a legitimate profit making business opportunity exists and inducing further investment.

*In re United Energy Corp.*, 944 F.2d at 596 citing *Cunningham v. Brown*, 265 U.S. at 7-8 (original Ponzi decision); *Securities Investor Protection Corporation v. Bernard L. Madoff Investment Securities, LLC (In re Bernard L. Madoff Investment Securities, LLC)*, 424 B.R. 122, 128, 141 (Bankr. S.D.N.Y. 2010)("Rather than engage in legitimate trading activity, Madoff used customer funds to support operations and fulfill other investors' requests for distributions of profits to perpetuate his Ponzi scheme. Thus, any payment of 'profit' to a BLMIS customer came from another BLMIS customer's initial investment"); *Eberhard v. Marcu*, 530 F.3d 122, 132 n. 7 (2d Cir. 2008)(describing a Ponzi scheme as "where earlier investors are paid from the investments of more recent investors...until the scheme ceases to attract new investors and the pyramid collapses");

*Official Committee of Unsecured Creditors v. R.F. Lafferty & Co., Inc., et al.*, 267 F.3d at 343-44; *In re Slatkin*, 525 F.3d at 813-14.

With this definition in mind, we can identify the cause of the "Ponzi scheme problem" and how it impacts fraudulent transfer claims – in a Ponzi scheme, the debtor entity that is used as the vehicle to perpetrate the scheme is operating in a continuing cycle of insolvency and deception, often from the beginning, which means that payments made by the debtor to investors are by definition made when the debtor is insolvent and are made with intent to hinder, delay and defraud creditors through the use of misappropriated funds to maintain the façade of profit and success and to further conceal and perpetuate the scheme. This type of fraud was described by Chief Justice Taft in the original Ponzi decision when he wrote - "[h]e [Charles Ponzi] was always insolvent, and became daily more so, the more his business succeeded. He made no investments of any kind, so that all the money he had at any time was solely the result of loans by his dupes". *Cunningham v. Brown*, 265 U.S. at 8.

In an effort to recover funds for the benefit of all duped investors, some of whom may have lost their entire investment, bankruptcy trustees or other plaintiffs will often file fraudulent transfer claims against investors who received payments, on one or more of the following grounds:

(1) all payments made to investors in a Ponzi scheme are presumptively made with actual intent to hinder, delay or defraud creditors of the debtor and therefore must be returned as intentional fraudulent transfers, regardless of the debtor's insolvency or whether reasonably equivalent value or fair consideration was received by the debtor in exchange; and/or

(2) because a Ponzi scheme debtor is always insolvent, and the payments made to the investors are made not from profits of the business but from money misappropriated from other investors, no reasonably equivalent value or fair consideration was ever received by the debtor in exchange for the investor payments and therefore the payments must be returned as constructive fraudulent transfers; and/or

(3) investors who receive payments from a Ponzi scheme debtor and who were on inquiry notice that a Ponzi scheme was being perpetrated, must return those payments as either intentional or constructive fraudulent transfers regardless of any value given in exchange because the payments were not received in good faith.

Most courts that have addressed these three arguments in Ponzi scheme cases appear to have allowed the trustee/plaintiff to recover the investor payments. However, the majority trend also appears to be that the trustee may recover *only* that portion of the payments that constituted interest or some other form of investment return that exceeded the investor's original principal amount. *SeeIn re Consolidated Meridian Funds a/k/a Meridian Investors Trust, et al.*, -- B.R. --, 2013 WL 366223 at *9; *In re United Energy Corp.*, 944 F.2d at 596; *In re Bayou*, 439 B.R. at 308-29; *In re Bernard L. Madoff Investment Securities, LLC*, 424 B.R. at 125, 135-36 (noting that the trustee had avoidance powers to deny claims filed by duped Ponzi scheme investors to the extent those claims exceeded the investors' "net equity investment", which equals the cash they deposited less amounts withdrawn). *See also Cunningham v. Brown*, 265 U.S. at 7-8;*In re National Audit Defense Network*, 367 B.R. at 221-23 (presence of a "Ponzi like" scheme was sufficient to establish defendants' intent to hinder, delay or defraud creditors).

Practitioners should note, however, that some courts differ on the issue of whether a trustee can recover payments made to duped Ponzi scheme investors and what the amount of that recovery should be. Contrary to the cases cited above, some courts have concluded that Ponzi scheme investors may keep all the payments they received from the Ponzi operator if the payments were made pursuant to a lawful contract between the Ponzi scheme operator and the investor, while yet other courts have concluded that Ponzi scheme investors may keep their original principal investment amounts, plus a reasonable, commercial rate of return, but must return as a fraudulent transfer any "outsized" portion of their return. *Lustig v. Weisz and Associates, Inc., et al. (In re Unified Commercial Capital, Inc.)*, 260 B.R. 343, 350 n.8 (Bankr. W. D. N.Y. 2001) (payments by debtor in Ponzi scheme case on a lawful contract constituted payment on account of an antecedent debt and therefore "value" was given by the investor, preventing such payments from being recoverable by the trustee as fraudulent transfers); *see also* In re *Carrozzella & Richardson,* 286 B.R. at 483-84, 487-92 (discussing the split of authority among courts in which some courts prohibit a Ponzi scheme investor from retaining any interest received on their investment because no reasonably equivalent value was received by the debtor, while others focus on the contract between the Ponzi operator and the investor and allow the investor to keep the payments as satisfaction of an antecedent debt); *Donell v. Kowell,* 533 F. 3d at 771-73 (summarizes Ninth Circuit rules used to determine when Ponzi scheme investors can be required to return as fraudulent transfers, payments received from the debtor); *In re Bayou Group, LLC et al.*, 439 B.R. at 304-29 (on a claim for intentional fraudulent transfer, the court applied an "inquiry notice" test to determine the good faith of the defendants who had received the transfers and reversed the bankruptcy court's granting of summary judgment in favor of the trustee, concluding that there were genuine issues of material fact presented for trial on the issue of the Ponzi scheme investors' good faith).

The law in this area is evolving and practitioners are best advised to consider all the above-described theories and to consult controlling legal authorities before filing or defending against fraudulent transfer claims that arise in Ponzi scheme cases.

# 17.

## The bar against constructive fraudulent transfer claims in § 546(e) of the Bankruptcy Code

Section 546(e) of the Bankruptcy Code bars a plaintiff from recovering, either under § 548 of the Bankruptcy Code or under state fraudulent transfer statutes pursuant to 11 U.S.C. § 544, transfers that fit the Bankruptcy Code's definitions of "margin payments" or "settlement payments" that were "made by or to (or for the benefit of) a commodity broker, forward contract merchant, stockbroker, financial institution, financial participant, or securities clearing agency, in connection with a securities contract...commodity contract..., or forward contract, that is made before the commencement of the case", unless the transfer is made with actual intent to hinder, delay or defraud creditors, as provided in 11 U.S.C. § 548(a)(1)(A); 11 U.S.C. § 546(e); *Bevill, Bresler & Schulman*

*Asset Management Corp. v. Spencer Savings & Loan Ass'n,* 878 F.2d 742, 751 (3d Cir. 1989); *Lowenschuss, etc. v. Resorts International, Inc. (In re Resorts International, Inc.),* 181 F.3d 505, 515 (3d Cir. 1999) ("*Resorts*"); *Bear Stearns Securities Corp. v. Gredd (In re Manhattan Investment Fund Ltd.),* 397 B.R. 1, 13 n.8 (S.D.N.Y. 2007); *In re Slatkin,* 525 F.3d 816-20.

Often referred to as the § 546(e) fraudulent transfer "safe harbor" provision, courts have interpreted this provision "extremely broadly", notably in cases involving "settlement payments". In *Resorts* (a leading case on the subject) the United States Court of Appeals for the Third Circuit held that the definition of "settlement payment" in § 546(e) is "extremely broad" and "may be the deposit of cash by the purchaser or the deposit or transfer of the securities by the dealer, and that it includes transfers which are normally regarded as part of the settlement process, whether they occur on the trade date, the scheduled settlement day, or any other date in the settlement process for the particular type of transaction at hand". *In re Resorts International, Inc.,* 181 F.3d at 515; *see also* *Enron Creditors Recovery Corp. v. ALFA, S.A.B. DE C.V. ING VP Balanced Portfolio, Inc.,* 651 F.3d 329, 334 (2d Cir. 2011) (payments made by Enron Corp. to redeem its own commercial paper before it matured were "settlement payments" under § 546(e) and therefore were shielded from avoidance); *Picard v. Katz*, 462 B.R. 447, 451-53 (S.D.N.Y. 2011) (payments made to customers of Bernard L. Madoff Investment Securities, LLC, were "settlement payments" protected from avoidance by the safe harbor of § 546(e)); *QSI Holdings, Inc. v. Alford* (*In re QSI Holdings, Inc.*), 571 F.3d 545, 548-50 (6th Cir. 2009).

Plaintiffs and defendants in actions involving claims for constructive fraudulent transfers brought under either § 548 of the Bankruptcy Code and/or under state law pursuant to the strong arm powers in § 544 of the Bankruptcy Code, should be well aware of the § 546(e) "safe harbor" exception and its extremely broad application. The law on the § 546(e) safe harbor is evolving and has had substantial treatment in the *Madoff* avoidance litigation. *E.g.*, *Picard v. Katz*, 462 B.R. at 451-53; *In re Bernard Madoff Investment Securities LLC*, 424 B.R. at 136-137, n. 30 (§ 546(e) safe harbor should not be used to lend judicial support to a Ponzi scheme such as the one Madoff was operating). Given this broad application, defendants are best advised to think creatively and to make full use of the § 546(e) "safe harbor" when warranted.

# 18.

**Is contribution or indemnification available?**

While there appears to be some agreement[26], for certain purposes, that fraudulent transfer claims are traditional torts (such as, for example, when courts apply conflicts of law principles to determine what state law applies to a fraudulent transfer claim), there appears to be no express agreement by the courts as to whether traditional tort concepts of contribution, indemnification and apportionment of liability among co-defendants, apply in fraudulent transfer cases. *SeeSecurities and Exchange Commission v. The Infinity Group Company*, 27 F.Supp.2d 559, 564 (E.D. Pa.

---

[26] The words "some agreement" may be too generous, as other courts have likened fraudulent transfer claims to state law contract claims, at least for purposes of determining which statute of limitations applies. *In re Century City Doctors Hospital, LLC*, 466 B.R. at 8-9 *citingStern v. Marshall*, 131 S. Ct. at 2614 *quotingGranfinanciera S.A. v. Nordberg*, 492 U.S. at 56.

1998); *RCA Corp. v. Tucker*, 696 F. Supp. 845, 853 (E.D.N.Y. 1988); *In re PWS Holding Corp.*, 228 F.3d at 240; *In re O'Day Corporation*, 126 B.R. at 391; *Pereira v. Dow Chemical Company (In re Trace International Holdings, Inc., et al.)*, 287 B.R. 98, 104-06 (Bankr. S.D.N.Y. 2002). The courts' relative silence on this issue is likely rooted in the requirement of fraudulent transfer law that a party must actually receive a transfer of the debtor's property, or benefit from such a transfer or an obligation incurred by the debtor, to be found liable. *In re Fedders North America, Inc.*, 405 B.R. at 548; *Edgewater Growth Capital Partners, L.P. v. H.I.G. Capital, Inc.*, -- A.3d --, 2010 Del. Ch. LEXIS 42 at *6-*7 (Del. 2010).

Hence, a defendant in a fraudulent transfer action can only be found liable if the plaintiff can prove that the defendant actually received a transfer of the debtor's property or benefitted from a transfer of the debtor's property or an obligation incurred by the debtor. The transfer or benefit must be identified, valued and traced to the defendant. Because of this requirement, there is typically no factual or legal basis to apply traditional concepts of joint and several liability or apportionment of fault among the defendants based on contribution, indemnification or some other concept of shared liability.[27] Either the defendant received a transfer or a benefit or it did not; and the defendant will only be liable for damages in an amount equal to the value of the property or benefit it actually received, nothing more, nothing less. *See* Rights of Indemnification and Contribution Among Persons Liable For Fraudulent Conveyances, 23 Seton Hall L. Rev. 1600 (1992-1993); *Wiebolt Stores, Inc. By and Through Raleigh v. Schottenstein*, 111 B.R. 167, 173 (N.D. Ill. 1990), *entry of final judgment* 1990 WL 60679 (N.D. Ill. 1990).

This requirement, that a defendant must receive a transfer of debtor property or benefit from a transfer or obligation of the debtor to be found liable on a fraudulent transfer claim, finds further recognition in the law of "aiding and abetting" – namely, most courts that have considered claims for aiding and abetting fraudulent transfers have concluded that no such claim exists absent the actual receipt of a transfer or benefit by the defendant. *In re Fedders North America, Inc.*, 405 B.R. at 548-549; *Chepstow Limited v. Hunt*, 381 F.3d 1077, 1089 (11th Cir. 2004); *Mann v. GTCR Golder Rauner, L.L.C.*, 483 F.Supp.2d 884, 918-19 (D. Az. 2007) (adopting majority view that there is no independent cause of action for aiding and abetting a fraudulent transfer under

---

[27] It should also be noted that there are no joint and several liability provisions in the fraudulent transfer sections of the Bankruptcy Code or in the UFTA or the UFCA. *E.g.,* 6 Del C § 1301, *et seq.*; Cal. Civ. Code § 3429.01, *et seq.*; New York Debtor and Creditor Law § 270, *et seq.*

the Arizona Uniform Fraudulent Transfer Act); *Trenwick America Litigation Trust v. Ernst & Young, L.L.P., et al.*, 906 A.2d 168, 203 and n. 97 (citing cases) (Del. Ch. 2006) ("Despite the breadth of remedies available under state and federal fraudulent conveyance statutes, those laws have not been interpreted as creating a cause of action for 'aiding and abetting'"); *Edgewater Growth Capital Partners, L.P., et al. v. Edgewater Private Equity Fund III, L.P., et al.*, --A.3d--, 2010 Del Ch. LEXIS 42 at *5-*8 (Delaware Fraudulent Transfer Act is identical to UFTA and explicitly provides a cause of action only against transferees and does not create a cause of action for aiding and abetting).

This *de facto* bar to traditional indemnification and contribution rights in fraudulent transfer cases, can likely be overcome only by a contractual right of contribution or indemnity. Absent such a contractual right, defendants in fraudulent transfer cases generally should not expect to be able to assert cross claims or third-party claims seeking indemnity or contribution.

# 19.

## Is there directors and officers liability insurance coverage?

Can a defendant in a fraudulent transfer case who was a director, officer or employee of a business at the time of the transfer or obligation, obtain insurance coverage and defense costs under the company's directors and officers ("D&O") liability insurance policy? While there is no universal answer to this question, in many cases the answer appears to be "no."[28]

Insurers can make a number of arguments to deny D&O insurance coverage in fraudulent transfer cases. For example, a D&O carrier may argue that a fraudulent transfer claim falls within a "fraud" or "profit and advantage" exclu-

---

[28] For purposes of this Chapter, I have assumed that the hypothetical defendant is an "insured" person under the D&O policy. Do not make this assumption in practice.

sion in the D&O policy. It might also argue that the receipt of a fraudulent transfer alone, without accompanying allegations and proof of wrongful or negligent conduct by the insured, does not constitute a "wrongful act" under the D&O policy and therefore the claim is not covered. An insurer could also take the position that the repayment of a fraudulent transfer is not a covered "loss" under a D&O policy. There is some support in case law for this last argument.

Some courts have held that repayment of a fraudulent transfer is "restitutionary" in nature and therefore does not constitute a "loss" under a D & O policy. *See, e.g.,In re TransTexas Gas Corp.*, 597 F.3d at 310-11 ("[p]ayments fraudulent as to creditors that must therefore be repaid due to bankruptcy court order is a disgorgement of ill-gotten gains and a restitutionary payment and is not an insurable 'loss' under the policy"); *Level 3 Communications, Inc. v. Federal Insurance Company*, 272 F. 3d 908, 910-11 (7th Cir. 2001)("'loss' within the meaning of an insurance contract does not include restoration of an ill-gotten gain"); *Ryerson, Inc. v. Federal Insurance Company*, 676 F. 3d 610, 612-13 (7th Cir. 2012); *Dobson v. Twin City Fire Insurance Company*, 2012 U.S. Dist. LEXIS 93823 at *4, *27 (C.D. Cal. 2012)(return of constructive or intentional fraudulent transfers by a defendant is restitutionary and is not a "loss" under the insurance policy).[29]

Insurers may also argue that a fraudulent transfer claim asserted by the representative of the debtor entity against a former director or officer of the debtor, violates the "insured v. insured" exclusion in a D & O policy. *Dobson v. Twin City Fire Insurance Company*, 2012 U.S. Dist. LEXIS 93823 at *32 (noting that the insurer raised the "insured v. insured" exclusion as a basis to deny coverage for a fraudulent transfer claim, however, the court in *Dobson* did not decide that issue in its opinion).

A defendant in a fraudulent transfer action should proceed on the assumption that it will face these and possibly other coverage arguments from a D&O insurer and is best advised to seek an early coverage evaluation and to engage separate insurance coverage counsel if necessary.

Alternatively, a defendant in a fraudulent transfer case may be able to obtain D&O insurance coverage based on other claims alleged against it contemporaneously with

---

[29]Query whether the Fifth Circuit's decision in *TransTexas* and the Central District of California's decision in *Dobson*, that the repayment of a fraudulent transfer is "restitutionary" (i.e., equitable) is correct. This conclusion seems to contradict the decision of the Supreme Court of the United States in *Granfinanciera,* in which the court concluded that a claim seeking to avoid and recover money damages for fraudulent transfers is a legal claim. *Granfinanciera, S.A., et al. v. Nordberg, et al., 492 U.S. at 48.* The court in *Granfinanciera* did not define or describe a monetary recovery on a fraudulent transfer claim as "restitutionary".

fraudulent transfer claims, such as a claim for breach of fiduciary duty, and to seek an allocation of insurance proceeds among covered and non-covered claims. *Dobson v. Twin City Fire Insurance Company*, 2012 U.S. Dist. LEXIS 93823 at *5, *53 (allocation between covered and uncovered claims); *Ryerson, Inc. v. Federal Insurance Company*, 676 at 613-14 ("A judgment or settlement in a fraud case could involve a combination of restitution and damages, and then the insurance company would be liable for the damages portion in accordance with the allocation formula in the policy"); *e.g., James D. Lyon, Chapter 7 Trustee of ClassicStar, LLC v. Ferguson, et al.* (*In re ClassicStar Mare Lease Litigation*), Civil Action No. 09-215-JMH, Docket No. 40 (E.D. Ky. 2009)(claims for breach of fiduciary duty accompanying claims for constructive and intentional fraudulent transfers); *Michaelson v. Golden Gate Private Equity, Inc., et al.* (*In re Appleseed's Intermediate Holdings, LLC, et al.*), Adversary No. 11-51847-KG, Docket No. 1 (Bankr. D. Del. 2011); *In re Bayou Group, LLC, et al.*, 439 B.R. at 293; *In re Mervyn's Holdings, LLC, et al.*, 426 B.R. at 497-98, 500-02.

If plausible, plaintiffs should develop and bring claims in tandem with fraudulent transfer claims that provide a basis for D&O insurance coverage and with it, an enhanced source of recovery.

# 20.

## The role of experts

Plaintiffs and defendants in fraudulent transfer litigation are both likely to need experts to do one or more of the following: (1) identify all avoidable and recoverable transfers or obligations; (2) identify the debtor's interest in the property transferred or obligation incurred; (3) trace the cash or other property transferred; (4) identify all transferees, subsequent transferees and beneficiaries of the transfer or obligation; (5) value all non-cash property transferred or obligations incurred; (6) value all non-cash property received by the debtor in exchange for the transfers or obligation and opine as to whether it constitutes "reasonably equivalent value" or "fair consideration"; and (7) opine on the insolvency or solvency of the debtor (under applicable tests) at the time of the transfers or obligation or as a result of the transfers or obligation. *E.g., In re Bayou Group, LLC, et al.*, 439 B.R. at 331-37 (expert addressed insolvency, tracing and other issues); *In reInternational Administrative Services, Inc.*, 408 F.3d at 702-03 (forensic accountants were engaged to identify all transfers and to perform an extensive tracing of cash through numerous entities around the world); *In re TWA*, 180 B.R. at 404-14 (expert valuation of a variety of airline assets, valuation of liabilities of the debtor, description of the debtor's business and industry at the time of the transfers); *In re National Audit Defense Network*, 367 B.R. at 214-16 (forensic accountant); *In re Trigem America Corp.*, 431 B.R. at 867 (valuation expert); *In re Tousa, Inc.*, 680 F.3d at 1304-12 (experts on real estate valuation, public accounting, insolvency); *In re the O'Day Corporation*, 126 B.R. at 400-01 (accounting experts in fraudulent transfer case under the UFCA).

Plaintiffs and defendants may also need to offer evidence from industry experts to explain relevant industry practices and conditions and to set the economic context of the debtor's business at the time of the transfers or obligations. *E.g.,In re TWA*, 180 B.R. at 412-14, 422-29; *In re TWA*, 134 F.3d at 191-198. If tax issues are presented, as they often are in cases involving investment schemes, a specialized tax expert may be required. *E.g.,James D. Lyon,*

*Chapter 7 Trustee of ClassicStar, LLC v. Ferguson, et al.* (*In re ClassicStar Mare Lease Litigation*), Civil Action No. 09-215-JMH, Docket No. 40 at 8, 44-45, 64-65 (E.D. Ky. 2009); see *William T. Romanowski and Julie I. Romanowski v. Commissioner of Internal Revenue*, United States Tax Court, T.C. Memo 2012-55 (T.C., February 20, 2013) (denial of income tax deductions taken pursuant to investment scheme involving ClassicStar, LLC).

Assuming the Federal Rules of Civil Procedure apply, experts designated to give opinions at trial in fraudulent transfer actions will be required to provide written reports and to give depositions during discovery. Fed. R. Civ. P. 26(a)(2). State court practice may vary. *E.g.*,Pa. R. Civ. P. 4003.5 (expert discovery conducted by interrogatory).

## 21.

### Jury trials vs. non-jury trials

The Seventh Amendment to the Constitution of the United Statesprovides:

> In Suits at common law, where the value in controversy shall exceed twenty dollars, the right of trial by jury shall be preserved.

Constitution of the United States, Amendment VII. The Supreme Court of the United States has consistently interpreted "suits at common law" to mean "suits in which legal rights were to be ascertained and determined, in contradistinction to those where equitable rights alone were recognized, and equitable remedies were administered". *Granfinanciera, S.A. v. Nordberg*, 492 U.S. at 41, citing *Parsons v. Bedford*, 3 Pet. 433, 447 (1830). Suits involving such "legal rights" include suits for the avoidance and recovery of monetary damages for fraudulent transfers brought in cases under the Bankruptcy Code in which the defendant has not filed a proof of claim against the debtor's estate. *Id.* at 55-57, 64-65; *Stern v. Marshall*, 131 S. Ct. at 2598-99; *see also Langenkamp v. Culp*, 498 U.S. 42, 45 (1990) (claim by trustee to recover a preferential transfer is a legal action for money damages to which the jury trial right attaches if the defendant has not filed a proof of claim in the debtor's bankruptcy case).

Assuming a jury trial right attaches, whether a party prefers to proceed with a jury trial or a non-jury trial in a fraudulent transfer case, will depend on the unique facts and circumstances presented and will likely involve many of the same considerations that bear on a party's decision to seek a jury or non-jury trial in any commercial case. A high degree of complexity may weigh against a jury for the plaintiff; it may weigh in favor of a jury for the defendant.

In fraudulent transfer cases filed in United States bankruptcy courts, if the jury trial right attaches, the bankruptcy court is not permitted to conduct the jury trial unless it is specifically designated to do so by the district court and only if all parties to the litigation consent. 28 U.S.C. § 157(e). A party who has a jury trial right in a bankruptcy case and who wants to protect that right, must file a timely jury demand in the manner prescribed by Fed. R. Civ. P. 38 or the right can be waived. Fed. R. Civ. P. 38; Fed. R. Bankr. P. 9015. If the bankruptcy court is specially designated by the district court to conduct jury trials, the parties can consent to have the jury trial before the bankruptcy judge by filing a joint or separate statements of consent within the time set by local rule. Fed. R. Bankr. P. 9015(b).

If the jury trial cannot be conducted in the bankruptcy court, then the party requesting the jury trial must file a timely motion with the district court seeking to withdraw the reference of the case to the bankruptcy court to have a jury trial in the district court. 28 U.S.C. §§ 157(a), (d). *See* Chapter 22, subsection a., "Withdrawal of the bankruptcy reference", *infra*.

A motion to withdraw the bankruptcy reference, when granted, will transfer the fraudulent transfer case from the bankruptcy court to the district court, although the case may not actually move from the bankruptcy court to the district court until the case is jury trial ready, which will not be until discovery is completed and summary judgment motions ruled upon. *In re Slatkin*, 525 F.3d at 811 (bankruptcy judge granting summary judgment did not deprive defendant of jury trial right).

However, transfer of the case from the bankruptcy court to the district court can also be immediate upon the granting of a motion to withdraw the reference. The decision on when withdrawal of the reference is actually effectuated is discretionary with the district court. *NDEP Corporation v. Handl-It, Inc. (In re NDEP Corporation)*, 203 B.R. 905, 908 (D. Del. 1996); *In re Appleseed's Intermediate Holdings, LLC, et al.*, 2011 U.S. Dist. LEXIS 14435 at *5-*11; *Official Committee of Unsecured Creditors, etc. v. Schwartzman, et al. (In re Stansbury Poplar Place, Inc.)*, 13 F.3d 122, 129 (4th Cir. 1993); *Gumport, etc. v. Growth Financial Corporation (In re Transcon Lines)*, 121 B.R. 837, 844-45 (C.D. Cal. 1990); *In re Consolidated Meridian Funds, a/k/a Meridian Investors Trust, et al.*, -- B.R. -- , 2013 WL 366223 at *2 (bankruptcy court can decide a motion for summary judgment even when a motion to withdraw the reference has been filed in the district court but not yet decided).[30] Once the case moves to the district court, it is handled in the same manner as any other civil jury case.

---

[30] For an example of jury instructions in a fraudulent transfer case *see James D. Lyon, Chapter 7 Trustee of ClassicStar, LLC v. Ferguson, et al. (In re ClassicStar Mare Lease Litigation)*, Civil Action No. 09-215-JMH, Docket No. 314 (E.D. Ky. 2011).

## 22.

**Bankruptcy courts vs. other courts**

Because they address fraudulent transfer claims frequently, it is probably safe to assume that United States bankruptcy courts are the courts most familiar with fraudulent transfer cases and the unique issues they present. Therefore, proceeding with a fraudulent transfer case in the bankruptcy court as opposed to another court, should result in less time spent on "learning curves" about concepts such as insolvency, asset valuation, financial issues and the like. Bankruptcy judges generally have more familiarity than non-bankruptcy judges with accounting, finance and similar subjects, which arise regularly in bankruptcy matters. Bankruptcy judges may also be less influenced by the apparent "innocence" of a fraudulent transfer defendant, who may have been sued for nothing more than receiving a transfer or other benefit from the debtor, but who otherwise did nothing "wrong". Motions in limine and other pre-trial matters are typically more limited in bankruptcy courts, where non-jury trials are the norm. From a defendant's perspective, bankruptcy courts are sometimes perceived as being "pro debtor" or "pro trustee" and may have a built-in sensitivity to the need of the debtor's estate to raise funds to pay for case administration, avoid administrative insolvency and to achieve a recovery for unsecured creditors, the constituency that benefits from fraudulent transfer recoveries. *SeeBuncher v. Official Committee of Unsecured Creditors of Genfarm LP IV*, 299 F.3d at 250.

United States district courts, or state courts, may, on the other hand, provide a superior forum for defendants in fraudulent transfer cases by removing the trustee's "home court advantage" and by "slowing down" the trustee with more formal process and pre-trial procedures. Less familiarity in the district court (or state court) with fraudulent transfer concepts, such as insolvency and financial and accounting issues that are the steady diet of bankruptcy judges, may also make non-bankruptcy courts more attractive to a defendant by reducing the trustee's knowledge advantage with the judge.

A jury of lay persons, whether in the bankruptcy court, the United States district court or in a state court, may provide a defendant in a fraudulent transfer case with a fresh, untainted audience with no built in pro-debtor or pro-trustee bias, or it may present an unpredictable wild card.

### a. Withdrawal of the bankruptcy reference

The United States district courts, *not* the bankruptcy courts, have "original and exclusive jurisdiction of all cases under title 11 [the Bankruptcy Code]" and "original but not exclusive jurisdiction of all civil proceedings arising under title 11, or arising in or related to cases under title 11". 28 U.S.C. § 1334(a). In each federal district, "the bankruptcy judges in regular active service shall constitute a unit of the district court to be known as the bankruptcy court for the district". 28 U.S.C. § 151. Each district court may enter an order providing "that any and all cases under title 11 and any and all proceedings arising under title 11 or arising in or related to a case under title 11 shall be referred to the bankruptcy judges for the district" (known as the "bankruptcy reference" or just the "reference"). 28 U.S.C. § 157(a). The district court, either on its own motion or on timely motion of a party, may withdraw, in whole or in part, any case or proceeding referred to the bankruptcy court for "cause shown" (called "discretionary withdrawal"). 28 U.S.C. § 157(d). The district court *shall* withdraw the bankruptcy reference "[i]f the court determines that resolution of the proceeding requires consideration of both title 11 and other laws of the United States regulating organizations or activities affecting interstate commerce" (called "mandatory withdrawal"). *Id.*

Thus, in appropriate cases, a defendant may have grounds to seek withdrawal of the bankruptcy reference for a trial in the district court. This can arise when, for example, a jury trial has been properly demanded by the defendant, the district court has not designated the bankruptcy court to conduct jury trials and the parties have not consented to a jury trial in the bankruptcy court. 28 U.S.C. 157(e); *e.g.In re Appleseed's Intermediate Holdings, LLC*, 2011 U.S. Dist. LEXIS 144315 at *5-*12; *In re NDEP Corporation*, 203 B.R. 905 at 907, 913-14 (discretionary withdrawal of the reference immediately granted due to jury trial right); *Sigma Micro Corporation v. Healthcentral.com (In re Healthcentral.com)*, 504 F. 3d 775, 786, 788 (9th Cir. 2007)(while the court determined that the defendant was entitled to a jury trial in the district court, discretionary withdrawal of the bankruptcy reference was delayed, allowing the case to remain with the bankruptcy court for all pre trial matters).

The bankruptcy reference can also be withdrawn when a federal statute regulating organizations or activities affecting interstate commerce must also be considered along with title 11. 11 U.S.C. § 157(d); *Securities Investor Protection Corporation v. Bernard L. Madoff Investment Securities LLC*, 2012 U.S. Dist. LEXIS 92230 at \*18-\*20 (S.D.N.Y. 2012).

Thus, if a party (typically a defendant) in a fraudulent transfer case properly and timely demands a jury trial, or can show some other basis for withdrawal of the bankruptcy reference, such as the need for the court to consider a federal statute in addition to title 11, that party must move promptly to have the bankruptcy reference withdrawn. Practitioners should be aware of local rules that govern motions to withdraw the bankruptcy reference, as they may determine when and where such motions must be filed. *E.g.*, Del. L. Bankr. Rule 5011-1 (provides that motions to withdraw the bankruptcy reference must be filed with the bankruptcy court and are then transmitted to the district court for decision). Some local rules can be onerous with respect to a party's right to seek withdrawal of the bankruptcy reference, even providing that a party can waive its right to seek withdrawal of the bankruptcy reference if the party does not file such a motion within the time prescribed by local rule. *E.g.* S.D.Ind. L. Bankr. R. 9015 (noting that the district court in the southern district of Indiana has designated the bankruptcy court to conduct jury trials and requiring a party who desires a jury trial in the district court, to move to withdraw the bankruptcy reference within 30 days after making a jury demand or that party is deemed to have waived their right to seek withdrawal of the bankruptcy reference).

# 23.

## A special problem – related criminal proceedings

Like other cases, fraudulent transfer litigation can be influenced by outside factors. One such outside factor could be the presence of an ongoing criminal grand jury investigation that targets former insiders of the debtor who are also defendants or witnesses in a fraudulent transfer action involving the same matters. If a grand jury has been impaneled and is investigating the pre-bankruptcy activities of the debtor and its insiders, this can hamper civil discovery in the fraudulent transfer case due to Fifth Amendment privilege assertions by individuals who are targets of the criminal investigation. Individuals who are targets of a criminal investigation who are also subject to discovery requests in a related civil action, may seek to stay civil discovery against them to avoid being forced to make the Hobson's choice of either refusing to testify in the civil action, thereby risking an inference of civil liability, or testifying in the civil action and thereby risk waiving their Fifth Amendment privilege against self-incrimination in the criminal matter. *West Hills Farms, LLC, et al. v. ClassicStar, LLC(In re ClassicStar Mare Lease Litigation)*, 823 F. Supp. 2d 599, 622 (E.D. Ky. 2011); *see also West Hills Farms LLC, et al. v. ClassicStar, LLC, et al. (In re ClassicStar Mare Lease Litigation)*, Civil Action No. 07-353, Docket No. 689 (E.D. Ky. 2008); *National Audit Defense Network*, 367 B.R. at 216-18.

A fraudulent transfer case can also be seriously impacted by guilty pleas or convictions in a related criminal case. If criminal convictions or guilty pleas are obtained during the pendency of a related fraudulent transfer case, those guilty pleas and convictions can be used against a defendant as evidence of actual intent to hinder, delay or defraud creditors or as admissions of fact helpful to the plaintiff, often with devastating effect. *United States v. Skinner*, 25 F. 3d 1314, 1316 (6th Cir. 1994)(quoting *McCarthy v. United States*, 394 U.S. 459, 466 (1969))("A guilty plea is an 'admission of all the elements of a formal criminal charge'...Thus, when a defendant pleads guilty, he admits and is estopped from relitigating the material facts in the information, and a plaintiff is entitled to introduce pleas from criminal cases in subsequent civil cases to establish 'all matters of fact and law necessarily decided by the conviction'"); *West Hills Farms, LLC, et al. v. ClassicStar, LLC, et al. (In re ClassicStar Mare Lease Litigation)*, 823 F. Supp. 2d at 622; *In re Bayou Group, LLC, et al.*, 439 B.R. at 306, 307; *In re Consolidated Meridian Funds a/k/a Meridian Investors Trust, et al.*, -- B.R.--, 2013 WL 366223 at *2; *In re The 1031 Tax Group, LLC*, 439 B.R. at 72 ("Moreover, courts readily accept admissions from guilty pleas of officers from companies involved in fraudulent activities as evidence that the fraud was a Ponzi scheme"); *Scholes v. Lehmann, et al.*, 56 F. 3d at 762 (plea agreements are admissible in civil cases under F.R.E. 803(22) and may be the subject of judicial notice under F.R.E. 201); *In re Slatkin*, 525 F.3d at 811-14 (guilty plea by perpetrator of a Ponzi scheme was admissible against him in a fraudulent transfer case pursuant to the F.R.E. 807 hearsay exception).

Plaintiffs and defendants should stay abreast of all relevant criminal matters and be aware of their potential impact on a related fraudulent transfer case.

# 24.

## Pre-complaint discovery under Fed. R. Bankr. P. 2004

Many of the strategies and tactics available to plaintiffs and defendants in fraudulent transfer litigation do not vary radically from those used in other complex commercial cases. However, some are unique. For example, a bankruptcy trustee, debtor-in-possession, court-appointed committee or other party-in-interest in a bankruptcy case, can take advantage of pre-complaint fact gathering available under Federal Rule of Bankruptcy Procedure 2004. Fed. R. Bankr. 2004 grants the estate representative or other party-in-interest in a bankruptcy case, wide latitude to gather documents and take testimony from witnesses on any matter that may affect the administration of the debtor's estate. Fed. R. Bankr. P. 2004. This would include gathering information to support claims by the estate arising from the debtor's pre-bankruptcy activities, such as facts relating to fraudulent transfer claims.

While information gathered under Fed. R. Bankr. P. 2004 technically is not a substitute for civil discovery, courts have interpreted Fed. R. Bankr. P. 2004 very broadly, providing that it permits a "fishing expedition" into all matters relevant to the bankruptcy case. *Dynamic Finance Corporation, et al. (In re North Plaza, LLC)*, 395 B.R. 113, 122, n.9 (C.D.Cal. 2008)("An examination under Bankruptcy Rule 2004 is nonadversarial in nature and aimed at discovering evidence upon which future causes of action may be based...and have been compared to 'fishing expeditions'");*In re Subpoena Duces Tecum etc., et al.*, 461 B.R. 823, 829 (Bankr. C.D. Cal. 2011); *In re Thomas L. Deshelter, et al.*, 453 B.R. 295, 302 (Bankr. S.D. Oh. 2011). *See, In re ClassicStar, LLC*, Debtor, Chapter 7, Case No. 07-51786-JAL, Docket Nos. 347, 351 (Bankr. E.D. Ky. 2009); *In re Summit Corp.*, 891 F.2d 1, 5 (1st Cir. 1989) (party bidding on debtor's assets is an interested party for purposes of Fed. R. Bankr. P. 2004(a)).

Prospective plaintiffs may also seek to use Fed. R. Bankr. P. 2004 for its other practical benefits such as to identify and authenticate documents and to identify parties and witnesses.

Prospective defendants subject to document requests and testimony under Fed. R. Bankr. P. 2004, may wish to use the process to convince the estate representative that there are no claims against them worth pursuing or to study the approach the plaintiff may take in subsequent litigation. It is not uncommon for local rules to permit parties to proceed with Rule 2004 discovery by agreement, without the need for a court order. *E.g.*, D. Del. Local Bankruptcy Rule 2004-1; E.D. Pa. Local Bankruptcy Rule 2004-1. Parties are best advised to reach agreement on Rule 2004 parameters to maintain better control over the process and to avoid burdening the court with matters that can be easily resolved by agreement.

# 25.

## Budgeting

As in all complex litigation, budgeting in fraudulent transfer cases can be difficult. Nevertheless, budget estimates meaningful to the client, counsel and to the entire litigation team, can be developed. Budget accuracy can be improved through early document review, fact building and legal research. If possible, preliminary cash or other asset tracing and an early insolvency evaluation with input from accountants or other experts, can improve budget accuracy, especially in cases that involve a large volume of transfers and transferees. *See, e.g., In re International Administrative Services, Inc.*, 408 F.3d at 702 (noting that trustee's forensic accountant "worked long and hard to discover all the intricacies of IAS' and Given's asset diversion plan"); *James D. Lyon, Chapter 7 Trustee of ClassicStar LLC v. Ferguson, et al.* (*In re ClassicStar Mare Lease Litigation*), Civil Action No. 09-215-JMH, Docket No. 40 at 55-66 (E.D. Ky. 2009).

Expert costs can be substantial in fraudulent transfer litigation, especially if complex money tracing, asset valuation and insolvency determinations are required. However, these expenses can be managed. Early involvement by the testifying experts will generally lead to better results and should help control costs over the long haul.

While every case is different, following is a list of budget categories that may be helpful. Not all of these categories will be relevant in every case:

- Initial legal research
- Initial document gathering with client
- Document preservation and electronic storage
- Identify all areas where expert assistance will be needed
- Identify and segregate transfer documents
- Identify and segregate money tracing documents
- Identify and segregate insolvency documents
- Identify and segregate other critical documents, e.g., letters, e-mails, memoranda, agreements, etc.
- Identify fact witnesses
- Interview available fact witnesses
- Review relevant materials from any related litigation
- Engage experts, i.e., consulting, testifying
- Pre-suit fact gathering under Fed. R. Bankr. P. 2004, if available

- Create discovery plan
- Discovery scheduling with client, opposing counsel and the court
- Jury trial evaluation, if available
- Draft, file and serve pleadings
- Motions to dismiss and accompanying briefs
- Other motions (e. g., withdrawal of the reference)
- Written fact discovery served, responded to
- Review and organize documents produced in fact discovery
- Prepare for, take and defend fact depositions
- Discovery motion practice
- Expert reports (opening and rebuttal)
- Expert discovery (i.e., work papers, other documents, depositions)
- Dispositive motions, i.e., summary judgment
- Create trial book
- Pre-trial conferences
- Trial scheduling and pre-trial deadlines
- Pre-trial order
- Marking and disclosure of all trial exhibits and witness lists
- Motions in limine
- Trial briefs
- Jury instructions
- Interrogatories to the jury, verdict forms
- Travel, conference room space, technology for trial, other trial logistics
- Trial preparation with witnesses, examination outlines, exhibits, review and run through
- Trial (all phases, i.e., opening, case-in-chief, direct, cross, rebuttal, sur-rebuttal, closing, motion for judgment as a matter of law, etc.)

- Post-trial matters
- Appeal (budget separately)

As all litigators know, bench trials are generally less time consuming and less expensive than jury trials and will not require a number of the items listed above. The parties may also stipulate to many of the facts and agree to the admissibility of many documentary exhibits, thereby reducing trial preparation work.

One issue that is often unique to fraudulent transfer litigation and which can seriously impact budgeting and trial preparation, is the issue of the debtor's insolvency. If insolvency is contested and is a required element of the plaintiff's *prima facie* case, then to avoid the costs of a full blown trial on all issues, the parties may wish to consider severing the issue of the debtor's insolvency and trying that issue first. *E.g.Braniff Insolvency Litigation (In re Braniff, Inc.)*, 1992 Bankr. LEXIS 1563 (Bankr. M.D. Fla. 1992).

Budgets for experts can be developed either separately or simultaneously with budgets for legal counsel, and while experts should be well involved with legal counsel early and often, generally speaking their budgets should be lower than the budgets for legal counsel.

As in other litigation matters, budgets in fraudulent transfer cases should be designed for flexibility and adjustment as the case proceeds.

# TABLE OF AUTHORITIES

**CASES**

*3V Capital Masters Fund, Ltd., et al. v. Official Committee of Unsecured Creditors of Tousa, Inc., et al. (In re Tousa, Inc.)*,
444 B.R. 613 (S.D. Fla. 2011) *rev'd at* 680 F.3d 1298 (11th Cir. 2012) ........................ 27, 28, 33, 36, 82, 112

*AFI Holding, Inc. v. Mackenzie*,
525 F.3d 700 (9th Cir. 2008) ..................................... 39 n.10

*Akande v. Transamerica Airlines, Inc. (In re Transamerica Airlines, Inc.)*,
2006 Del. Ch. LEXIS 47 (Del, Ch. 2006) ........................ 59

*Allard v. Flamingo Hilton (In re Chomakos)*,
69 F.3d 769 (6th Cir. 1995) ............................................. 34

*Appalachian Oil Company, Inc. v. The Virginian Travel Plaza, Inc. (In re Appalachian Oil Company, Inc.)*,
2011 WL 2565692 (Bankr. E.D. Tenn. 2011) .................. 81

*Ashcroft v. Iqbal*,
129 S. Ct. 1937 (2009) ............................................. 73, 74

*Askanase v. Fatjo*,
1993 WL 208682 (S.D. Tex. 1993) ........................ 85 n.22

*August v. August*,
2009 Del. Ch. LEXIS 21 (Del. Ch. 2009) .................... 13, 15

*Barber v. Gold Seed Co.*,
129 F.3d 382 (7th Cir. 1997) ............................................. 33

*Bear Stearns Securities Corp. v. Gredd (In re Manhattan Investment Fund Ltd.)*,
397 B.R. 1 (S.D.N.Y. 2007) ............................................. 101

*Begier v. I.R.S.*,
496 U.S. 53 (1990) ...................................................... 27, 29

*Belfance v. Bushey (In re Bushey)*,
210 B.R. 95 (6th Cir. B.A.P. 1997) ............................... 65, 85

*Bell Atlantic Corp. v. Twombly*,
550 U.S. 544 (2007) ................................................... 73, 74

*Best Manufacturing v. White Plains Coat and Apron Co. (In re Daniele Landries, Inc.)*,
40 B.R. 404 (Bankr. S.D.N.Y. 1984) ............................... 64

*Bevill, Bresler & Schulman Asset Management Corp. v. Spencer Savings & Loan Ass'n*,
878 F.2d 742 (3d Cir. 1989) ......................................... 100

*BFP v. Resolution Trust Corp.*,
511 U.S. 531 (1994) .................................................. 34, 83

*Black & White Cattle Co. v. Granada Cattle Services, Inc. (In re Black & White Cattle Co.)*,
783 F.2d 1454 (9th Cir. 1986) ........................................ 22

*Board of Teamsters Local 863 Pension Fund v. Foodtown, Inc.*,
296 F.3d 164 (3d Cir. 2002) ............................................ 64

*Brandt v. B.A. Capital Company LP (In re Plassein Int'l. Corp., et al.)*,
366 B.R. 318 (Bankr D. Del. 2007) ............................. 23, 81

*Braunstein v. Walsh (In re Rowanoak Corp.)*,
344 F.3d 126 (1st Cir. 2003) ........................................... 36

*Breeden v. L.I. Bridge Fund, LLC (In re Bennett Funding Corp.),*
232 B.R. 565 (Bankr. N.D.N.Y. 1999) .............................. 87

*Buncher v. Official Committee of Unsecured Creditors of Genfarm LP IV,*
229 F. 3d 245 (3d Cir. 2000) ........................... 11, 14, 119

*Butler Aviation International v. White (In re Fairchild Aircraft Corp.),*
6 F.3d 1119 (5th Cir. 1993) ................................................ 34

*Butner v. United States,*
440 U.S. 48 (1979) ............................................................ 28

*Caplin v. Marine Midland Trust Co.,*
406 U.S. 416 (1972) .......................................................... 66

*Charys Liquidating Trust, etc. v. McMahan Securities Co., L.P. (In re Charys Holding Company, Inc.),*
443 B.R. 628 (Bankr. D. Del. 2010) .................... 52 n.14, 75

*Chepstow Limited v. Hunt,*
381 F.3d 1077 (11th Cir. 2004) ....................................... 105

*Childs v. Brandon,*
90 A. D. 2d 983 (N.Y. App. Div. 4th Dep't 1982) .............. 55

*Christian Brothers High School Endowment v. Bayou No Leverage Fund, LLC, et al. (In re Bayou Group, LLC, et al.),*
439 B.R. 284 (S.D.N.Y. 2010) ................................. passim

*Christy v. Alexander & Alexander of New York, Inc., et al. (In re Finley, Kumble, et al.),*
130 F.3d 52 (2d Cir. 1997) ................................... 31 n.9, 82

*Coffey v. Foamex, L.P.*,
  2 F.3d 157 (6th Cir. 1993) .................................................. 16

*Coleman v. Home Savings Association* (*In re Coleman*),
  21 B.R. 832 (Bankr. S.D. Tex. 1982) ........... 44, 63 n.18, 88

*Committee of Unsecured Creditors for Pittsburgh Cut Flower Company, Inc. v. Hoopes* (*In re Pittsburgh Cut Flower Company, Inc.*),
  124 B.R. 451 (Bankr. W.D. Pa. 1991) .......................... 21 n.7

*Constructora Maza, Inc. v. Banco de Ponce*,
  616 F.2d 573 (1st Cir. 1980) ............................................. 46

*Cooper v. Ashley Communications* (*In re Morris Communications NC, Inc.*),
  914 F.2d 458 (4th Cir. 1990) ............................................ 32

*Cooper v. Centar Investments (Asia) Ltd., et al.* (*In re Trigem America Corporation*),
  431 B.R. 855 (Bankr. C.D. Cal. 2010) ....................... 29, 112

*Corbin v. Franklin National Bank* (*In re Franklin National Bank Securities Litigation*),
  2 B.R. 687 (E.D.N.Y. 1979) .............................................. 46

*Covey v. Commercial National Bank of Peoria*,
  960 F. 2d 657 (7th Cir. 1992) ........................................... 44

*Cunningham v. Brown, et al.*,
  265 U.S. 1 (1924) ................................... 39 n.10, 50, 94, 95

*Dahar v. Jackson* (*In re Jackson*),
  459 F.3d 117 (1st Cir. 2006) ............................................ 36

*Daley, et al. v. Zofia Deptula, et al. (In re Carrozzella & Richardson),*
   286 B.R. 480 (D. Conn. 2002) ...................... 39, 69, 85, 98

*Diamond v. Friedman (In re Century City Doctors Hospital, LLC),*
   466 B.R. 1 (Bankr. C.D. Cal. 2012) ........... 79, 85, 103 n. 26

*Dobson v. Twin City Fire Insurance Company,*
   2012 U.S. Dist. LEXIS 93823 (C.D. Cal. 2012) ..... 108, 109

*Donell v. Kowell,*
   533 F.3d 762 (9th Cir. 2008) ........................ 52 n.14, 62, 98

*Durrett v. Washington National Ins. Co.,*
   621 F.2d 201 (5th Cir. 1980) ........................................... 35

*EBC I, Inc. v. America Online Inc. (In re EBC I, Inc., et al.),*
   356 B.R. 631 (Bankr. D. Del. 2006) ............................... 28

*Eberhard v. Marcu,*
   530 F.3d 122 (2d Cir. 2008) ............................................ 94

*Edgewater Growth Capital Partners, L.P. v. H.I.G. Capital, Inc.,*
   -- A.3d --, 2010 Del. Ch. LEXIS 42 (Del. 2010) .... 104, 106

*End of the Road Trust, ex rel. Freuhauf Trailer Corp. v. Terex Corp. (In re Freuhauf Trailer Corporation),*
   250 B.R. 168 (D. Del. 2000) ....................................... 59, 61

*Enron Creditors Recovery Corp. v. ALFA, S.A.B. DE C.V. ING VP Balanced Portfolio, Inc.,*
   651 F.3d 329 (2d Cir. 2011) ........................................... 101

*Feldman v. Chase Home Finance (In re Image Masters, Inc.),*
421 B.R. 164 (Bankr. E.D. Pa. 2009)............................... 75

*First Federal of Michigan v. Barrow,*
878 F.2d 912 (6th Cir. 1989) ........................................... 49

*Fleming Companies, Inc. v. Rich,*
978 F. Supp. 1281 (E.D. Mo. 1997)........................... 41, 82

*Friedman v. Wahrsager,*
848 F. Supp. 278 (E.D.N.Y. 2012) ................................... 64

*G.E. Credit Corp. v. Murphy(In re Rodriguez),*
895 F.2d 725 (11th Cir. 1990).............................................12

*Gillardi v. Henry,*
113 S.W.2d 1158 (Ky. 1938) ............................................ 54

*Global Link Liquidating Trust, etc. v. Avantel, S.A. (In re Global Link Telecom Corp., et al.),*
327 B.R. 711 (Bankr. D. Del. 2005) ......................... passim

*Golden v. The Guardian (In re Lenox Healthcare, Inc.),*
343 B.R. 96 (Bankr. D. Del. 2006)............................28, 30

*Goldman Sachs Execution & Clearing, L.P., et al. v. The Official Unsecured Creditors Committee of Bayou Group, LLC, et al.,*
2012 U.S. App. LEXIS 13531 (2d Cir. 2012) ............. 31 n.9

*Gordon v. Kinney (In re Gallagher),*
417 B.R. 677 (Bankr. W.D.N.Y. 2009) .......................... 44

*Granfinanciera, S.A. v. Nordberg,*
492 U.S. 33 (1989).................... 12, 103 n. 26, 109 n.29, 114

*Gumport, etc. v. Growth Financial Corporation* (*In re Transcon Lines*),
121 B.R. 837 (C.D. Cal. 1990) .......................................... 117

*Hall v. Walter* (*In re Hall*),
139 F.3d 911 (10th Cir. 1998).............................................. 64

*Harbinger Capital Partners Master Fund I, Ltd. v. Granite Broadcasting Corp., et al.*,
906 A. 2d 218 (Del. Ch. 2006) ................................. 52 n.14

*Harris v. National Investment Finance Company Inc.* (*In re Akin*),
64 B.R. 510 (Bankr. W.D. Ky. 1986) ............................... 85

*Haskell v. PWS Holding Corporation* (*In re PWS Holding Corporation, et al.*),
303 F. 3d 308 (3d Cir. 2002) *cert. denied*,
*Haskell v. PWS Holding Corp.*, 123 S Ct. 1594
(2003) ............................................................ 11, 62, 64, 104

*Hassett v. McColley* (*In re O.P.M. Leasing Services, Inc., et al.*),
28 B.R. 740 (Bankr. S.D.N.Y. 1983)................................. 65

*Hayes v. Palm Seedlings Partners-A* (*In re Agricultural Research and Technology Group, Inc.*),
916 F.2d 528 (9th Cir. 1990) .............................. 52 n.14, 87

*HBE Leasing Corp. v. Frank*,
48 F.3d 623 (2d Cir. 1995) ............................................... 35

*Hechinger Investment Co. of DE v. Fleet Retail Finance Group* (*In reHechinger Investment Co. of DE*),
327 B.R. 537 (Bankr. D. Del. 2005) ................................ 23

*Helig-Meyers Co. v. Wachovia Bank, N.A.(In re Helig-Meyers Co.),*
328 B.R. 471 (E.D. Va. 2005) .......................................... 44

*Holmberg v. Armbrecht,*
327 U.S. 392 (1946) ......................................................... 59

*Howdeshell of Ft. Myers v. Dunham-Bush, Inc. (In re Howdeshell of Fort Myers),*
55 B.R. 470 (Bankr. M.D. Fla. 1985) .............................. 29

*IBT International, Inc., et al. v. Northern (In re International Administrative Services, Inc.),*
408 F.3d 689 (11th Cir. 2008) ................................. passim

*In re Appleseed's Intermediate Holdings, LLC et al.,*Chapter 11, Case No. 11-10160-KG, Joint Plan of Reorganization, etc., Docket No. 683 (Bankr. D. Del. 2011) ........................................................................ 62

*In re ClassicStar, LLC, Debtor, Chapter 7 Case No. 07-51786-JAL, Docket Nos. 347, 351 (Bankr. E.D. Ky. 2009) ........................................................................ 128*

*In re Subpoena Duces Tecum etc., et al.,*
461 B.R. 823 (Bankr. C.D. Cal. 2011) .......................... 128

*In re Summit Corp.,*
891 F.2d 1 (1st Cir. 1989) .............................................. 128

*In re Thomas L. Deshelter, et al.,*
453 B.R. 295 (Bankr. S.D. Oh. 2011) ........................... 128

*In re Xonics Photochemical, Inc.,*
841 F.2d 198 (7th Cir. 1988) ........................................... 45

*Industrial Enterprises of America, Inc. v. Burtis, et al.* (*In re Pitt Penn Holding Co.*),
2012 Bankr. LEXIS 325 (Bankr. D. Del. 2012) ........ 57 n.16

*Jacoway v. Anderson, et al.* (*In re Ozark Restaurant Equipment Co.*),
850 F.2d 342 (8th Cir. 1988) .......................................... 34

*James D. Lyon, Chapter 7 Trustee of ClassicStar, LLC v. Ferguson, et al.* (*In re ClassicStar Mare Lease Litigation*),
Civil Action No. 09-215-JHM, Docket No. 314 (E.D. Ky. 2011) ........................................................ 117 n.30

*James D. Lyon, Chapter 7 Trustee of ClassicStar LLC v. Ferguson, et al.* (*In re ClassicStar Mare Lease Litigation*),
Civil Action No. 09-215-JMH, Docket No. 40 (E.D. Ky. 2009) ........................................ 50, 64, 68, 77, 110, 112

*Johnson, et al. v. Neilson* (*In re Slatkin*),
525 F.3d 805 (9th Cir. 2008) ................................... *passim*

*Joseph v. Frank, et al. (In re Troll Communications)*,
385 B.R. 110 (Bankr. D. Del. 2008). No .......................... 40

*Kapila v. Espirito Santo Bank* (*In re Bankfest Capital Corp.*),
374 B.R. 333 (Bankr. S.D. Fla. 2007) .............................. 29

*Kendall v. Sorani (In re Richmond Produce Co.)*,
151 B.R. 1012 (Bankr. N.D. Cal. 1993) *aff'd*, 195 B.R. 455 (N.D. Cal. 1996) ............................................. 45

*Langenkamp v. Culp*,
498 U.S. 42 (1990) ....................................................... 115

*Leonard v. Coolidge, et al. (In re National Audit Defense Network),*
367 B.R. 207 (Bankr. D. Nev. 2007) ........................ *passim*

*Level 3 Communications, Inc. v. Federal Insurance Company,*
272 F. 3d 908 (7th Cir. 2001) .......................................... 108

*Lids Corporation v. Marathon Investment Partners, L.P. (In re Lids Corp.),*
281 B.R. 535 (Bankr. D. Del. 2002) ................................ 45

*Lippe, et al. v. Bairnco Corporation,*
249 F. Supp. 2d 357 (S.D.N.Y. 2003) .............................. 46

*Lisle v. John Wiley & Sons, Inc. (In reWilkinson, et al.),*
196 Fed. Appx. 337 (6th Cir. 2006) ................................ 34

*Lowenschuss, etc. v. Resorts International, Inc. (In re Resorts International, Inc.),*
181 F.3d 505 (3d Cir. 1999) ........................................... 101

*Lustig v. Weisz and Associates, Inc., et al. (In re Unified Commercial Capital, Inc.),*
260 B.R. 343 (Bankr. W. D. N.Y. 2001) ......................... 98

*Lyon v. Contech Construction Products, Inc. (In re Computrex, Inc.),*
403 F.3d 807 (6th Cir. 2005) ........................ 30, 30 n.8, 81

*Mann v. GTCR Golder Rauner, L.L.C.,*
483 F.Supp.2d 884 (D. Az. 2007) ................................. 105

*Max Sugarman v. A.D.B. Investors, et al.,*
926 F.2d 1248 (1st Cir. 1991) ................................... 12, 42

*McHale v. Boulder Capital, LLC, et al. (In re The 1031 Exchange Group LLC, et al.),*
439 B.R. 47 (Bankr. S.D.N.Y. 2010)..........................27, 124

*Melamed v. Lake County National Bank,*
727 F.2d 1399 (6th Cir. 1974)................................................ 16

*Mellon Bank, N.A. v. Official Committee of Unsecured Creditors of R.M.L., Inc. (In re R.M.L., Inc.),*
92 F.3d 139 (3d Cir. 1996)..................................................... 32

*Mendelsohn v. Jacobwitz, et al. (In re Jacobs),*
394 B.R. 646 (Bankr. E.D.N.Y. 2008) ............... 36, 43 n.12

*Merrill v. Abbott (In re Independent Clearing House Company),*
77 B.R. 843 (D. Utah 1987) ..........................39 n.10, 64, 80

*Mervyn's Holdings, LLC v. Lubert-Adler Group IV, LLC (In re Mervyn's Holdings, LLC),*
426 B.R. 488 (Bankr. D. Del. 2010).........................73, 110

*Michaelson, as Trustee of the Appleseed's Litigation Trust v. Golden Gate Equity, Inc. et al. (In re Appleseed's Intermediate Holdings, LLC, et al.),*
Adversary No. 11-51847-KG, Docket No. 1 at 12-16 (Bankr. D. Del. 2011).........................................................17

*Michaelson v. Golden Gate Private Equity, Inc., et al. (In re Appleseed's Intermediate Holdings, Inc., et al.),* 2011 U.S. Dist. Lexis 144315
(D. Del. 2011)................................................. 89, 91, 117, 121

*Mitchell v. Wilmington Trust Co.,*
449 A.2d 1055 (Del. Ch. 1982) .........................................20

*Murphy v. Meritor Savings Bank (In re O'Day Corporation),*
   126 B.R. 370 (Bank. D. Mass. 1991) ........................ passim

*National Labor Relations Board v. Arsham,*
   873 F.2d 884 (6th Cir. 1989).................................12, 65, 85

*National Loan Investors, L.P. v. LAN Associates XII, LLP,*
   2002 Conn. Super. LEXIS 2233 (Conn. Super. Ct. 2002) ..............................................................................21 n.7

*National Tax Credit Partners, L.P. v. Havlik,*
   20 F. 3d 705 (7th Cir. 1994) ............................................. 63

*NDEP Corporation v. Handl-It, Inc. (In re NDEP Corporation),*
   203 B.R. 905 (D. Del. 1996) ..................................... 115, 119

*Nordberg v. Sanchez (In re Chase & Sanborn Corp.),*
   813 F.2d 1177 (11th Cir. 1987)............................................ 29

*Official Committee of Unsecured Creditors, etc. v. Schwartzman, et al. (In re Stansbury Poplar Place, Inc.),*
   13 F.3d 122 (4th Cir. 1993) ............................................. 117

*Official Committee of Unsecured Creditors of Fedders North America, Inc., et al. v. Goldman Sachs Credit Partners, L.P., et al. (In re Fedders North America, Inc., et al.),*
   405 B.R. 527 (Bankr. D. Del. 2009) ........................ passim

*Official Committee of Unsecured Creditors of Midway Games, Inc. v. National Amusements, Inc. (In re Midway Games, Inc.),*
   428 B.R. 303 (Bankr. D. Del. 2010)................................ 42

*Official Committee of Unsecured Creditors v. Pardee (In re Stanwich Financial Services Corp.)*,
291 B.R. 25 (Bankr. D. Conn. 2003) ....................... 58 n.16

*Official Committee of Unsecured Creditors v. R.F. Lafferty & Co., Inc., et al.*,
267 F.2d 340 (3d Cir. 2001) ........................................ 63, 94

*Official Committee of Unsecured Creditors of Verestar, Inc. v. Am. Tower Corp. (In re Verestar, Inc.)*,
343 B.R. 444 (Bankr. S.D.N.Y 2006) .............................. 39

*Ogden v. Big Sky Motors, Ltd.*,
314 F. 3d 1190 (10th Cir. 2002) ........................... 29, 31 n.9

*OHC Liquidating Trust v. Nucor Corp. (In re Oakwood Homes Corp.)*,
325 B.R. 696 (Bankr. D. Del. 2005) ............................... 75

*Osage Crude Oil Purchasing, Inc. v. Osage Oil and Transportation, Inc. (In re Osage Crude Oil Purchasing, Inc.)*,
103 B.R. 256 (Bankr. N. D. Okla. 1989) .................... 23, 24

*Paloian v. American Express Co. (In re Canopy Financial, Inc.)*,
2011 WL 3911082 (D. N.D. Ill. 2011) ............................. 92

*Paloian v. LaSalle Bank, N.A.*,
619 F. 2d 688 (7thCir. 2010) ..................................... 31 n.9

*Pardo v. Avanti Corporate Health System (In re APF Co.)*,
274 B.R. 634 (Bankr. D. Del. 2001) ........... 40, 60, 85 n.22

*Pereira v. Dow Chemical Company (In re Trace International Holdings, Inc., et al.)*,
287 B.R. 98 (Bankr. S.D.N.Y. 2002) .............................. 104

*Pergrem v. Smith*,
255 S.W.2d 42 (Ky. 1953) ................................................. 54

*Picard v. Katz*,
462 B.R. 447 (S.D.N.Y. 2011) ......................................... 102

*Plotkin v. Pomona Valley Imports, Inc. (In re Cohen)*,
199 B.R. 709 (9th Cir. 1996) ...................................... 40 n.10

*QSI Holdings, Inc. v. Alford (In re QSI Holdings, Inc.)*,
571 F.3d 545 (6th Cir. 2009) ........................................... 102

*RCA Corp. v. Tucker*,
696 F. Supp. 845 (E.D.N.Y. 1988) ................................. 104

*Richards v. Jones*,
142 A. 832 (Del. 1928) ....................................................... 65

*Rubin v. Manufacturers Hanover Trust Co.*,
661 F.2d 979 (2d Cir. 1981) ....................................... 23, 34

*Ryerson, Inc. v. Federal Insurance Company*,
676 F. 3d 610 (7th Cir. 2012) .................................. 108, 110

*Schilling v. Heavrin (In re Triple S Restaurants, Inc.)*,
422 F.3d 405 (6th Cir. 2005) ..................................... 41 n.11

*Schock v. Nash*,
732 A.2d 217 (Del. 1999) .................................................. 13

*Scholes v. Lehmann et al.*,
56 F.3d 750 (7th Cir. 1995) ....................................... 46, 126

*Securities and Exchange Commission v. The Infinity Group Company,*
27 F.Supp.2d 559 (E.D. Pa. 1998) .................................. 103

*Securities Investor Protection Corporation v. Bernard L. Madoff Investment Securities, LLC (In re Bernard L. Madoff Investment Securities, LLC),*
424 B.R. 122 (Bankr. S.D.N.Y. 2010) ................ 94, 97, 102

*Securities Investor Protection Corporation v. Bernard L. Madoff Investment Securities LLC,*
2012 U.S. Dist. LEXIS 92230 (S.D.N.Y. 2012) ............. 120

*Segal v. Rochelle,*
382 U.S. 375 (1966) ......................................................... 27

*Sharp International Corp v. State Street Bank and Trust (In re Sharp International Corp.),*
403 F.3d 43 (2d Cir. 2005) ...................................... passim

*Sigma Micro Corporation v. Healthcentral.com (In re Healthcentral.com),*
504 F. 3d 775 (9th Cir. 2007) ......................................... 119

*Stanley v. U.S. Bank, National Association (In re TransTexas Gas Corp.),*
597 F.3d 298 (5th Cir. 2010) ..................................... passim

*Stern v. Marshall,*
131 S. Ct. 2594 (2011) ............................. 90, 103 n. 26, 115

*Stoebner v. Consumer Energy Company (In re LGI Energy Solutions, Inc., et al.),*
460 B.R. 720 (8th Cir. B.A.P. 2011) ................................ 30

*The Official Committee of Unsecured Creditors of Cybergenics Corporation, et al. v. Chinery, et al. (In re Cybergenics Corporation),*
330 F.3d 548 (3d Cir. 2003) ............................................. 63

*Thrifty Dutchman, Inc. v. Florida Supermarkets, Inc. (In re Thrifty Dutchman, Inc.),*
97 B.R. 101 (Bankr. S.D. Fla. 1998) ................................. 35

*Tiab Communications Corp. v. Keymarket of NEPA, Inc., et al.,*
263 F. Supp. 2d 925 (M.D. Pa. 2003) ............................... 16

*Travelers Casualty & Surety Co. of America v. Pacific Gas & Elec. Co.,*
549 U.S. 443 (1979) ......................................................... 28

*Trenwick America Litigation Trust v. Ernst & Young, L.L.P., et al.,*
906 A.2d 168, 203 and n. 97 (Del. Ch. 2006) ................. 106

*TSIC, Inc., etc. v. Thalheimer (In re TSIC, Inc.),*
428 B.R. 103 (Bankr. D. Del. 2010) ......................... 67 n.19

*TWA v. Travelers International AG (In re TWA),*
180 B.R. 389 (Bankr. D. Del. 1994) *rev'd and aff'd in part,* 134 F.3d 188 (3d Cir. 1998) .................... 36, 45, 112

*TWA v. Travellers International AG (In re TWA),*
134 F.3d 188 (3d Cir. 1998) ...................................... 44, 84

*U.S. Express Lines, Ltd. v. Higgins,*
281 F.3d 383 (3d Cir. 2002) ............................................ 73

*United States v. Gleneagles Inv. Co., et al.*, 565 F. Supp. 556 (M.D. Pa. 1983) *aff'd sub nom.*, *United States v. Tabor Court Realty Corp.*, 803 F. 2d 1288 (3d Cir. 1986), *cert. denied* 483 U.S. 1005 (1987) ..................................................................40, 46

*United States v. Green*,
201 F.3d 251 (3d Cir. 2000) ............................................. 20

*United States v. Hansel*,
999 F. Supp. 694 (N.D.N.Y 1998) ................................... 46

*United States v. Skinner*,
25 F. 3d 1314 (6th Cir. 1994) .........................................125

*United States v. Tabor Court Realty Corp., et al.*,
803 F. 2d 1288 (3d Cir. 1986) ......................................... 23

*United States v. Whiting Pools, Inc.*,
462 U.S. 198 (1983) ......................................................... 27

*VFB LLC v. Campbell Soup Co.*,
482 F.2d 624 (3d Cir. 2007) ............................................ 83

*Viscount Air Services, Inc. v. Cole, et al. (In re Viscount Air Services, Inc.)*,
232 B.R. 416 (Bankr. D. Az. 1998) ................................. 35

*Voest-Alpine Trading USA Corp. v. Vantage Steel Corp.*,
919 F.2d 206 (3d Cir. 1990) .......................................15, 23

*Wahoski v. Classic Packaging Co. (In re Pillowtex Corporation)*,
427 B.R. 301 (Bankr. D. Del. 2010) ................................ 75

*Walker v. South Central Bell Tel. Co.*,
904 F.2d 275 (5th Cir. 1990) ................................... 85 n.22

*Weiner v. A.G. Minzer Supply Corp. (In re UDI Corporation),*
301 B.R. 104 (Bankr. D. Mass. 2003.) ...................... 30 n.8

*Wellman v. Wellman,*
933 F.2d 215 (4th Cir. 1991) *cert. denied,* 502 U.S. 925 (1991) ........................................................................ 64

*West Hills Farms, LLC, et al. v. ClassicStar, LLC(In re ClassicStar Mare Lease Litigation),*
823 F. Supp. 2d 599 (E.D. Ky. 2011) ...................... 125, 126

*West Hills Farms LLC, et al. v. ClassicStar, LLC, et al. (In re ClassicStar Mare Lease Litigation),*
Civil Action No. 07-353, Docket No. 689 (E.D. Ky. 2008) ........................................................................... 125

*Wiebolt Stores, Inc. By and Through Raleigh v. Schottenstein,*
111 B.R. 167 (N.D. Ill. 1990) .......................................... 105

*William T. Romanowski and Julie I. Romanowski v. Commissioner of Internal Revenue,* United States Tax Court, T.C. Memo 2012-55 (T.C. February 20, 2013) ........................................................................... 113

*Wiscovitch-Rentas v. Venancio Marti Santa, et al. (In re Laser Realty, Inc.),*
2011 WL 2292269 (Bankr. P.R. 2011) ............................ 12

*Wyle v. C.H. Rider & Family (In reUnited Energy Corp.),*
944 F.2d 589 (9th Cir. 1991) ............................... 34, 94, 97

*Youngstown Osteopathic Hospital Association v. Pathways Center for Geriatric Psychiatry, Inc., et al.(In re Youngstown Osteopathic Hospital Association),*
280 B.R. 400 (Bankr. N.D. Oh. 2002) ............................ 71

**STATUTES AND RULES**

California Uniform Fraudulent Transfer Act, Cal. Civ. Code § 3439.01, *et seq.* ............................................ *passim*

Constitution of the United States, Amendment VII ............................................................... 114

Del. Ch. Rule 3 (aa) ............................................................. 74

Del. L. Bankr. R. 5011-1 ..................................................... 122

Delaware Uniform Fraudulent Transfer Act, 6 Del. C. § 1301, *et seq.* ........................................................ *passim*

Federal Rules of Bankruptcy Procedure ............................................................... *passim*

Federal Rules of Civil Procedure ............................................................... *passim*

Federal Rules of Evidence ....................................... 41 n.11, 126

Kentucky Fraudulent Conveyance Statute, Kentucky Revised Statutes §§ 378.010, 413.30 .................... 52, 53, 55

Massachusetts Uniform Fraudulent Transfer Act, Massachusetts General Law ch. 109A, § 5(b)(2010) ................... 20 n.6, 41 n.11, 68 n.20

New York Debtor and Creditor Law, § 270, *et seq.* ....... *passim*

Pennsylvania Rules of Civil Procedure .......................... 74, 113

Pennsylvania Uniform Fraudulent Transfer Act, 12 Pa.
 C.S. § 5101, *et seq*..................................................... *passim*

S.D. Ind. L. Bankr. R. 9015 ................................................ 122

United States Bankruptcy Code,
 11 U.S.C. § 101, *et seq*.............................................. *passim*

United States Judiciary Act, 28 U.S.C. § 1, *et seq*......... *passim*

## OTHER AUTHORITIES

American Bar Association, Section on Business Law,
 Report to the House Delegates, February 2013 .............. 91

Black's Law Dictionary (5th Ed. 1979).................................... 24

Collier On Bankruptcy ..................................... 16, 21 n.7, 27, 39

Rights of Indemnification and Contribution Among
 Persons Liable For Fraudulent Conveyances, 23
 Seton Hall L. Rev. 1600 (1992-1993) ........................... 105

The Black Swan, The Impact of the Highly Improbable
 (2d Ed. 2010), Nassim Nicholas Taleb ................... 93 n. 25

## INDEX

§ 548 of the Bankruptcy Code, 18, 53, 54, 59, 60, 92, 100, 102
§ 548 of the United States Bankruptcy Code, 2, 3, 4
70% benchmark rule, 34
accountants, 49, 50, 77, 112, 130
accounting records, 50
aiding and abetting, 105
allocation of insurance proceeds, 110
American Bar Association, 91
antecedent debt, 32, 33, 68, 98
appeal, 91, 133
apportionment of liability, 103
*Ashcroft v. Iqbal*, 129 S. Ct. 1937, 1949 (2009), 73
asset, 12, 49, 130, 131
assets, 2, 11, 13, 41, 44, 45, 46, 49, 64, 74, 112, 128
attorney's fees, 70
badge of fraud, 4, 40, 42, 46, 83, 84
badges of fraud, 3, 16, 20, 39, 40, 77, 82
Bankruptcy Code, 27, 28, 32, 43, 49, 52, 53, 57, 58, 60, 62, 70, 80, 84, 85, 87, 100, 115 120
bankruptcy court, 5, 7, 64, 91, 99, 108, 115, 116, 118, 120, 121, 122
bankruptcy judge, 89, 90, 91, 116
bankruptcy reference, 7, 116, 120, 121, 122
*Bayou Group, LLC*, 12, 15, 20, 39, 41, 65, 77, 78, 84, 87, 88, 89, 98, 110, 112, 126
bench trials, 133
benefit the debtor's unsecured creditors, 15
Black Swan, 93
breach of fiduciary duty, 110
budget estimates, 130
budgeting, 8, 130
burden of proving, 21, 36, 46, 47, 59, 87
California Uniform Fraudulent Transfer Act, 12
*Carrozzella & Richardson*, 39, 69, 85, 98
chapter 11 trustee, 62
chapter 7 trustee, 63, 64
*ClassicStar Mare Lease Litigation*, 50, 63, 64,

66, 68, 77, 110, 113, 117, 125, 126, 131
collapse multiple transfers, 23
common law fraud, 2, 16, 74, 75
complaint, 5, 8, 17, 61, 73, 76, 80, 81, 85, 90, 127
complaints, 5, 73, 75, 77
consent to the entry of final orders or judgments, 90, 91
constructive fraudulent transfer, 3, 17
contingent liabilities, 45
contribution, 6, 103, 104, 106
control, 28, 30, 31, 36, 50, 81, 129, 131
conviction, 126
convictions, 7, 41, 125
core proceedings, 89, 90, 91
courts most familiar with fraudulent transfer cases, 118
creditors, 2, 3, 4, 11, 12, 13, 14, 15, 16, 19, 29, 33, 38, 39, 41, 42, 43, 49, 61, 63, 64, 66, 75, 82, 85, 95, 96, 97, 100, 108, 119, 125
criminal grand jury, 124
criminal guilty pleas, 7, 41

criminal investigation, 7, 124
cross claims, 106
*Cunningham v. Brown, et al.*, 39, 50
D&O insurance, 109
debtor-in-possession, 13, 60, 62, 64, 65, 127
defending, 5, 15, 31, 79, 99
Del. L. Bankr. Rule 5011-1, 122
Delaware Uniform Fraudulent Transfer Act, 12
depositions, 113, 132
directors and officers, 6, 107
directors and officers liability insurance, 6, 107
earmarking, 29, 31
elements of a fraudulent transfer, 18
elements of intentional and constructive fraudulent transfer, 2
equitable tolling, 5, 19, 57, 58, 59, 60, 61, 80
execution, 72
expert, 4, 6, 7, 36, 47, 50, 77, 111, 112, 113, 130, 131, 133
fair consideration, 3, 14, 17, 19, 20, 21, 23, 24, 32,

33, 35, 36, 38, 41, 43, 55,
76, 79, 83, 89, 96, 111
fair value, 44
Fed. R. Bankr. 2004, 127
Fed. R. Civ. P., 47, 72, 73,
75, 90, 113, 116
Federal Rules of Civil
Procedure, 73, 113
Fifth Amendment
privilege, 7, 124
final orders and
judgments, 5, 89, 91
financial intermediary, 29,
31, 81
fishing expedition, 128
forensic accountant, 49,
50, 77, 112, 130
fraud, 2, 3, 4, 11, 12, 13, 15,
16, 17, 20, 21, 38, 39, 40,
41, 42, 46, 47, 54, 55, 74,
76, 77, 82, 83, 84, 88,
94, 95, 107, 110, 126
fraudulent transfer, 1, 2, 3,
4, 5, 6, 7, 8, 11, 12, 13, 14,
15, 16, 17, 18, 19, 20, 21,
23, 24, 27, 28, 29, 31,
33, 36, 38, 40, 42, 43,
45, 46, 49, 52, 53, 54,
55, 57, 58, 59, 60, 61, 62,
63, 64, 67, 68, 70, 72,
73, 74, 76, 77, 79, 80, 81,
82, 83, 84, 85, 87, 88,
90, 93, 95, 96, 98, 99,
100, 101, 102, 103, 104,
105, 106, 107, 109, 111,
113, 115, 116, 117, 118,
119, 120, 122, 124, 125,
127, 130, 131
GAAP, 45
goal, 11, 12, 64
goal of fraudulent transfer
law, 11
going-concern, 44
good faith, 5, 23, 33, 36,
55, 68, 76, 83, 87, 88,
89, 96, 99
good faith defense, 5, 79,
88
grand jury, 124
*Granfinanciera, S.A. v.
Nordberg*, 12, 103, 114
guilty pleas, 125
hinder, delay or defraud, 3,
4, 13, 15, 16, 19, 21, 38,
39, 42, 43, 82, 96, 97,
100, 125
ill-gotten gains, 108
immediate or mediate
transferee, 48, 88
indemnification, 6, 103,
104, 106
indemnity, 106
inference of civil liability,
125
initial transferee, 31, 48,
67, 68, 69, 71, 76, 88
inquiry notice, 87, 96, 99
insider, 20, 71, 77
insiders, 41, 54, 67, 68, 124

insolvency, 4, 20, 24, 41, 42, 43, 45, 46, 47, 77, 84, 95, 96, 111, 118, 119, 130, 131, 133, 161
insolvent, 14, 17, 19, 20, 21, 39, 43, 44, 83, 87, 95, 96
insurance, 6, 107, 109
insured v. insured, 109
intent to hinder, delay or defraud, 14, 39, 40
intentional fraudulent transfer claims, 3
interest of the debtor in property, 18, 26, 81, 82
investors, 94, 95, 96, 97
*Iqbal*, 73, 74
joint and several liability, 104, 105
jurisdiction, 120
jury, 7, 114, 115, 116, 117, 120, 121, 122, 124, 132, 133
jury instructions, 117, 132
jury trials, 7, 114, 116, 119, 121, 123, 133
liabilities, 44, 45, 112
limitations periods, 4, 24, 57
liquidating trust, 62
liquidation value, 44
local rule, 116, 122
local rules, 47, 122, 129
look back, 54

loss, 108
*Lyon*, 30, 50, 63, 64, 66, 68, 71, 77, 110, 112, 117, 130
*Madoff*, 94, 97, 102, 122
margin payments, 100
Massachusetts, General Law ch. 109A, 20, 41, 68
mere conduit, 29, 31, 82
misnomer, 2, 11, 12, 13
motion to withdraw the bankruptcy reference, 116
motions in limine, 119, 132
New York Debtor and Creditor Law, 13, 19, 21, 35, 39, 44, 46, 52, 53, 54, 55, 70, 79, 83, 89, 105
non-cash property, 111
non-core proceedings, 89
non-jury, 7, 114, 115, 119
obligation, 2, 3, 4, 14, 17, 18, 19, 21, 22, 23, 24, 26, 33, 36, 38, 41, 42, 43, 45, 54, 55, 59, 67, 74, 76, 80, 83, 84, 85, 86, 87, 104, 107, 111
obligations, 12, 17, 24, 25, 38, 53, 57, 58, 60, 80, 82, 111, 112
official committees, 61, 63
particularity requirement, 75

Pennsylvania Uniform Fraudulent Transfer Act, 13
plaintiff's *prima facie* case, 5, 47, 79, 80, 83
pleading, 5, 40, 73, 74, 75, 76, 90
Ponzi, 2, 6, 39, 41, 43, 77, 93, 94, 95, 96, 97, 99, 102, 126
post judgment interest, 71
pre and post judgment interest, 71
pre-complaint discovery, 8
present fair saleable value, 45, 46
pre-suit fact gathering under Fed. R. Bankr. P. 2004, 131
profit and advantage, 107
property, 3, 4, 12, 14, 15, 18, 22, 26, 28, 29, 30, 31, 32, 34, 35, 36, 38, 43, 48, 63, 69, 70, 76, 81, 89, 104, 105, 111
property of the debtor, 3, 26, 30, 63, 82
punitive damages, 70
reach back, 4, 54, 55, 57, 58, 59, 60, 80
reach back period, 4, 24, 54, 55, 57, 58, 59, 80
reasonably equivalent value, 3, 14, 17, 19, 20, 24, 32, 33, 35, 36, 38, 41, 76, 83, 96, 98, 111
receive a transfer, 14, 104
receiver, 62, 70
remedies, 70, 106, 114
remedy, 49
restitutionary, 108, 109
Rule 2004 of the Federal Rules of Bankruptcy Procedure, 8
S.D.Ind. L. Bankr. R. 9015, 122
safe harbor provision of § 546(e) of the United States Bankruptcy Code, 6, 101, 102
securities contract, 100
settlement payments, 100, 101
Seventh Amendment to the Constitution of the United States, 114
severing the issue of the debtor's insolvency, 133
standing, 5, 40, 63, 65, 84, 85
standing to sue, 5, 79, 84
state court, 7, 47, 74, 113, 119, 120, 161
state law, 4, 17, 18, 19, 28, 52, 55, 57, 58, 59, 60, 65, 79, 80, 84, 90, 91, 102, 103

statute of limitations, 5, 54, 55, 57, 59, 60, 79
*Stern v. Marshall*, 131 S. Ct. 2595 (2011), 6
strong arm power, 65
subsequent transferee, 48, 67, 71, 76, 88
summary judgment, 72, 99, 116, 117, 132
Supreme Court of the United States, 34, 90, 109, 114, 161
tax, 50, 112
third-party claims, 106
*Tousa*, 27, 28, 33, 36, 78, 112
tracing, 4, 48, 49
transfer, 2, 3, 4, 5, 7, 12, 13, 14, 15, 16, 18, 19, 20, 21, 22, 24, 26, 27, 28, 33, 36, 38, 41, 42, 43, 45, 48, 49, 50, 52, 53, 54, 55, 58, 59, 60, 61, 63, 64, 65, 68, 69, 70, 72, 74, 76, 80, 81, 83, 84, 85, 87, 88, 90, 99, 100, 101, 103, 104, 105, 107, 109, 111, 115, 116, 119, 124, 128
transferee, 4, 31, 36, 48, 55, 67, 68, 69, 71, 76, 81, 83, 87, 88, 89
transferor, 38, 39, 41, 64
*TWA*, 36, 44, 45, 84, 112

*Twombly*, 73, 74
UFCA, 18, 19, 21, 23, 24, 35, 36, 45, 46, 53, 80, 85, 105, 112
UFTA, 18, 22, 23, 27, 35, 36, 43, 48, 53, 54, 55, 59, 67, 70, 80, 85, 105, 106
Uniform Fraudulent Conveyance Act, 2, 3, 12, 18, 85
Uniform Fraudulent Transfer Act, 2, 3, 12, 18, 85, 106
United States Bankruptcy Code, 2, 3, 4, 6, 12, 161
United States bankruptcy courts, 7, 115, 118
United States Court of Appeals for the Ninth Circuit, 94
United States Court of Appeals for the Third Circuit, 101
United States district courts, 7, 119, 120
United States Tax Court, 113
unsecured creditors, 2, 11, 15, 34
valuation, 44
value, 2, 3, 14, 20, 25, 26, 32, 33, 35, 36, 45, 48, 55, 68, 70, 76, 83, 87,

88, 89, 96, 98, 105, 111, 114

withdrawal of the reference, 117, 121, 132

wrongful act, 108

## About the Author

Earl M. Forte is a partner at the law firm of Eckert Seamans Cherin & Mellott, LLC and is a member of the firm's Litigation, Business Counseling and Bankruptcy groups. He has substantial experience in corporate litigation, bankruptcy litigation and other insolvency and business disputes, including fraudulent transfer matters. Mr. Forte has been practicing law enthusiastically for over 30 years and represents a wide variety of clients. This is Mr. Forte's first book, which he originally published in 2013 and re-published in 2017. *See* www.amazon.com. For more information about Mr. Forte and and his law firm see Eckert Seaman's website at www.eckertseamans.com.

www.ingramcontent.com/pod-product-compliance
Lightning Source LLC
Chambersburg PA
CBHW021413210526
45463CB00001B/348